GREAT LITTLE RAILWAYS

RUSSELL CHAMBERLIN   COLIN GARRATT   PETER HILLMORE
SIMON HOGGART   STANLEY REYNOLDS   LYN WEBSTER   MICHAEL WOOD

GREAT LITTLE RAILWAYS

British Broadcasting Corporation

Published by the
British Broadcasting Corporation
35 Marylebone High Street
London W1M 4AA

First Published 1984

ISBN 0 563 20211 4

© The Contributors and the British Broadcasting Corporation 1984

Printed in England by
Jolly & Barber Ltd
Rugby, Warwickshire

Jacket by Glynn Boyd Harte

Contents

Introduction

COLIN ADAMS

Like many schoolboys in the fifties, I went train spotting complete with butties, bottle of water and notebook. It was not a particularly strong love affair, and I could barely tell one type of locomotive from another. But I did know that I preferred to catch sight of an engine number through the swirling steam of the early fifties rather than the diesel fug of later years.

My really close association with the railway business began twenty years later when I moved to Manchester for the BBC. We bought our house in a hurry – and soon lay abed under our new roof. As sleep began to claim us, we were disturbed by a steady and mounting rumble that ended in a fearsome whoosh. We had discovered what the estate agent had forgotten to mention. Our near-neighbour was the Manchester–London main line. I can now tell a local DMU from an inter-city 125 at a distance of 300 yards, with my eyes closed, and merely by the sound that the central heating radiators are making.

Despite this new-found expertise, when I inherited the idea of a series on narrow-gauge railways, I approached the task with some trepidation. I took home some books, discovered that the narrow gauge had originated in the slate quarries of North Wales, had been quickly adopted around the world, often as a cheap and rapid means of laying track, and that many of the lines were just as rapidly disappearing from the railway maps of the world. The series was under way. Producers set off in search of pictures and found misadventure. In the Philippines, Derek Towers had his knee in plaster after an accident on the footplate of a haunted locomotive. Bill Lyons journeyed to South America and collided with the Falklands factor. Brian James went to Portugal and discovered a national rail strike. Meanwhile, in India Gerry Troyna was still filling in forms. . . .

Eventually pictures started to come in. Of engines like the Shay, the Mogul 260, and the big, black Consolidation that carried Stanley Reynolds on his pilgrimage to Quito. Images of the vast, open fields of rural Poland under a hot summer sky . . . the meandering, verdant path of the Douro, Portugal's 'river of gold' . . . the evil, almost human Devil's Nose in Ecuador.

And then there were the people. Men like engineer J.D. True, who broke his pelvis when he and his locomotive toppled down one of the cliffs on the White Pass and Yukon railroad . . . Conrado Gabriel, telling in matter-of-fact tones how dozens of Filipino railmen were crushed by a runaway train . . . and the bewhiskered and bewitching O.P. Dixit, servant of Indian railways for forty years, and a detective on the Marudhar Express. For eighteen months they were our constant companions in the film cutting-rooms of BBC Manchester. Then, for seven weeks, they flickered across the TV screens of the nation. This book is a more tangible reminder of their stories and their achievements, of the final frontiers of make-do-and-mend railroading. Of those Great Little Railways.

Colin Adams
Executive producer
November 1983

THE YUKON
The Gold Rush Line
SIMON HOGGART

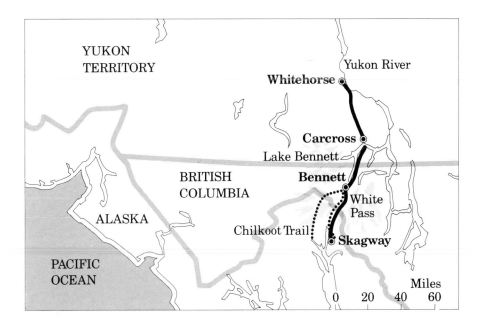

Much of the British Commonwealth is now embalmed for me in the pages of *The Children's Encyclopedia*, edited of course by Arthur Mee, whose twelve volumes were an endless treat to be enjoyed whenever I visited my grandparents. There was no nonsense here about losing an Empire and failing to find a role; in these thick and glossy pages Britain remained, in every sense, the centre of the world. The greatest glory, the clinching proof of our importance, was the Empire. You could find everything in the Empire. In more recent American books you encounter the same obsession with variety, with the extraordinary contrasts and wonders to be found across their country. In the days when it was we who had the limitless self-confidence, we found the same thing in our Empire. There were women who lengthened their necks with rings, people picking cotton in Egypt, Indians washing in the Ganges, Australians on sheep farms the size of Holland, pearl divers off the coral islands, African children in shirts and ties playing cricket under palm trees. These powerful evocations of the sheer size of the place – and thus our overwhelming pre-eminence in the world – were illustrated by stirring full-page paintings reproduced in black and white. These were somehow more satisfying than the smudgy photographs which were dotted elsewhere in the text and the improbable tints of the few colour pages. Underneath each painting was a caption carved rather than written, in the heroic style. 'Canadian Mounties always get their man. Here a sergeant in the North-west Mounted Police searches the snows of the Yukon Territory looking for a seemingly insignificant trace which will lead him towards the track of the miscreant he seeks. Mounties do not know the meaning of the word failure.' The last sentence I read literally, assuming that it had been cunningly concealed from them in order to make them more efficient policemen. The Mountie's jawline would be set against the gleaming wastes, and even his huskies would look eager, for in the British Empire of those days dogs too knew their duty, and did it, willingly.

I suppose our images of such distant places are usually like this, a set of snapshots like those dusty picture postcards sold in antique fairs. Other pictures were later dropped into the mental box labelled 'Yukon': Jack London's novels, Robert Service's evocative doggerel verse, the occasional short story about Mounties or fur trappers. When I arrived in the Yukon, twenty-five years after I had first heard of it, the most surprising discovery was that the image was largely true.

The Yukon reveals itself quite slowly. You land at a perfectly ordinary airport in an ordinary Canadian Pacific 737, and get a hire car into Whitehorse, a perfectly ordinary and slightly shabby North American town. There are drugstores, gas stations, offices, motels and cocktail lounges where homely young women have been put into sheath dresses with slit thighs so that they look like New York call girls, just as cocktail waitresses look in Oshkosh, Saskatoon, and indeed everywhere in North America except New York.

The first thing that tells you that the Yukon is different is its size, and this you learn soon. Most towns in the world have tendrils which stretch out towards other settlements: roads, bus routes, suburbs, telegraph wires. There are roads out of Whitehorse, though not very many, and the inhabited area ceases very quickly. Indeed, most of the town is literally trackless waste, because of the way in which the Yukon used to be administered. Unlike the Provinces in Canada, all the land here belonged to the Federal Government, so in order to have some land of their own the City threw an absurdly wide municipal limit around itself, so creating temporarily the largest, though one of the less populated, cities in Canada. In parts of the Whitehorse municipality you could walk for miles without seeing another human being.

We drove for a long time to find the next town, or at least what looked like a town on the map. It was called Jake's Corner, and turned out when we got there to be nothing but a filling station, a café and a dance hall, all of them built by the original Jake. He was a black-bearded Russian whose wife kept goats in the kitchen. The café is decorated in what must have been a chic style some years ago, with towelling on the tables and intercoms so that guests at one table can talk to those at another without walking across. The dance floor is suspended over a swimming pool. On busy nights people drive for a hundred miles to get here and sway briefly above the chlorine. Jake finally ran off with one of his waitresses, possibly to California, though nobody knows and in a way nobody cares since certainty would spoil the legend. If Jake didn't like your face he wouldn't serve you petrol, which was a serious matter on the Alaska Highway. He used to offer free ice-cream with purchases of a certain amount of petrol, though he once beat up a Swiss tourist who demanded it. At least I'm told he did; myths are important here and are lovingly passed on.

Even stranger is Dawson, which used to be the capital of the Yukon and was once, at the height of the Gold Rush, the biggest city west of Winnipeg. Dawson was the reason that they built the railway which we had come to visit. It stands on the confluence of the Yukon River and a wide stream which Indians called the 'Thron Duick', the name for their method of catching salmon by hammering stakes into the river bed. The white man corrupted this to 'Klondike', and it was on one of its small tributaries that gold was discovered here in 1896. For its size, the Klondike was probably the richest land on earth. Nobody is quite clear why, but one theory is that the ground tilted at some stage in prehistory, crushing a mother-lode of gold, then concentrating it by shaking and sluicing into one small patch of land. Here it was discovered by George Carmack, a white man who had married a squaw, and who was tracking disconsolately through the wilderness with some of his Indian relatives. He promptly blazed a gash on a spruce tree and claimed two five-hundred-foot stretches of the bed of the creek for himself. In exactly the same way present-day prospectors make their claims. The Klondike Gold Rush had begun.

What was slightly puzzling about the men who were searching for gold was their attitude towards it. They wanted gold – indeed they were driven to seek it – but they didn't really want wealth. They thought they did of course, but when they had it they scarcely knew what to do with it. The

Main Street, Dawson, during the Gold Rush, *c.* 1898

world first heard of the gold strike a year later when the first prospectors landed in Seattle on the steamer *Portland*. There were sixty-eight men on board, and they had a total of $700,000 worth of gold between them. Astonished reporters saw the stuff 'piled around the stateroom like so much valueless baggage'. But this was hardly surprising. One of the curious things about gold is that after a while it becomes to its seekers so much cold metal. A few hotels, shops and restaurants in the Yukon still accept gold in payment (and the banks have gold-dust counters, as ours have *bureaux de change*), and a prospector will often pay with a handsome nugget worth far more than the goods he has bought. A Whitehorse restaurateur described a customer who had given a favourite waitress a nugget worth hundreds of dollars because he liked the way she smiled. Some friends had a quantity of dust pressed on them in exchange for a lift, the gold being worth many times the cost of the petrol. Until recently, a miner in Dawson would happily leave thousands of dollars' worth unattended in an unlocked cabin.

But it isn't really wealth and fortune which make people come here. The big companies, who have taken over most of the old claims and operate them with vast modern plant, make plenty of money. But nobody comes here to wander over the inhospitable land because they really believe they will become rich. People go for the joy of the hunt or because they are trying to escape from something: a bad marriage, a sense of failure, from themselves. Even nowadays, as the prospecting season ends in September, you can watch miners gamble away their last gold at Diamond Tooth Gertie's, the only legal casino in Canada. At other times you may see them wrestling with the huge official surveys of the area, with all the excited certainty of a football fan who thinks he has found next week's score draws. Around October the snow begins to fall and the ground becomes too hard to dig. The 800 or so inhabitants of Dawson (every year young people of the type who used to be called hippies arrive and resolve to make the town their permanent home; most of them leave when the air turns chilly in autumn) turn back in on themselves. They like each other in this town; there are forty or so societies which flourish in the winter. 'It's good to go into a bar and know everyone inside', a local said to me. They make their money in the three months of summer and enjoy themselves for the other nine.

Dawson is now tiny, almost forgotten, but the railway it caused lives on. When news of the discovery in the Klondike reached the outside world by way of the steamers it was found that there were really only three ways into the goldfield. There was the all-water route which meant floating down the Yukon River through Alaska. That was slow and expensive, as well as chancy, for as winter approached, the waterways froze over quickly. There was the all-land route through Northern Canada, but this was appallingly difficult and dangerous. And there was the most popular route. This involved taking a steamer from California or Washington State and landing on what is now the Alaska Panhandle, at the minute ports of Skagway or Dyea. From here you walked the forty miles over the mountains to the head of Lake Bennett. Then in the summer months when the ice broke you could begin the long trip down the Yukon River to the goldfields. There were three snags about this hike. First, both passes, the Chilkoot from Dyea and the White Pass from Skagway, were exceedingly steep. Secondly, so that you might be ready for the thaw, the walk had to be done in winter, when 500 inches of snow is not uncommon on the passes. Finally, you did not simply have to do the walk once but as many as twenty times. This was because the Canadian Government sagaciously insisted that no one would be allowed to cross the border on the way to the Klondike without a year's supply of food and equipment. This generally weighed around a ton. Some people could afford to buy pack animals, which they grossly abused. Stampeders claimed that they saw horses and ponies commit suicide by stepping off the path rather than suffer under the weight they had to carry and the torture of the mosquitoes. Those who had no animals had to carry

Jeff's Place, Skagway, Soapy Smith's headquarters. This became a famous 'fleecing' place for 'suckers'

the goods themselves, time and time again, caching each bundle at the summit, where the Canadian border guards maintained their precarious authority with machine guns. They also, incidentally, charged a heavy duty on equipment bought in the United States, a source of much resentment at the time, though it seems reasonable enough since anyone could stake a claim in Canada, whereas only American citizens could do so in the US. The Mounties also confiscated side arms, which is largely why Dawson, in Canada, was at the height of the Gold Rush one of the most law-abiding towns on the continent, whereas Skagway, in the words of one Mountie, was 'little better than a hell on earth'.

At the time the stampeders began to arrive on the steamers, Skagway was, to all intents and purposes, run by Jefferson 'Soapy' Smith, a celebrated con-man who soon after his premature death became the town's leading tourist attraction. A native of Georgia, Smith soon realised that there was more money to be made more easily from the thousands of hopeful prospectors pouring through the town than there ever would be from the goldfields. As the new arrivals (known as 'cheechakos') docked they would find Smith on the quayside hustling soap. They would give him $5 – two days' wages for a labourer – in the vain hope of getting a bar with a hundred-dollar bill wrapped round it. Soon Smith found even simpler and more efficient ways of relieving the newcomers of their cash. His telegraph office would send a wire anywhere in the world, through an impressive looking cable which ran into the sea. There it abruptly stopped. Nevertheless

Tens of thousands begin the weary trek to the goldfields of the Yukon during the Gold Rush in 1896

anyone who sent a wire could expect a reply – collect. Smith ran all the rackets in town, of which there were many, and his men were quite prepared to cause a rock slide on the trail so that they might work fresh swindles on the prospectors thus detained. When war broke out between the US and Spain, Smith raised and drilled 400 'volunteers' whose services he offered to the President. When they were refused, he naturally kept them under arms for his own use at home.

By late 1897, the trails over the mountains had become entirely clogged with the stampeders. Anyone who left the plodding human chain for a rest might have to wait for hours until he regained his place. There were several schemes for improving the routes. George Brackett, a former railway engineer from Minneapolis, began the Skagway & Yukon Transportation and Improvement Company which was to build a wagon road over the

White Pass. He ran out of money in December of 1897, and though he returned the next summer, it was clear that something more substantial would be needed.

The idea for the railway was agreed, legend has it, in the bar of the St James Hotel, Skagway, early in 1898. Here Sir Thomas Tancrede, an Englishman who represented a group of British financiers, met Michael Heney, one of the most able and well-known railway engineers of his day. Tancrede, who had come north in order to discover whether a railway could be built, had surveyed the ground and concluded, not unreasonably, that it was impossible. Heney thought differently, and in the small hours of the morning persuaded Tancrede to produce the capital. They bought the right of way from Brackett, for a small fraction of his investment. One of their first decisions was to use a narrow gauge for the track. The standard gauge, as used in Britain, is 4 feet $8\frac{1}{2}$ inches, a peculiar width allegedly chosen because it was the distance at which Roman chariot wheels were set apart – though there is no clear evidence for this. Heney and Tancrede decided on 3 feet. The narrow gauge is particularly suitable for mountainous terrain, and the much smaller roadbed required makes it a great deal cheaper. The decision probably halved the cost of building the line. The engines and rolling stock are, however, normal size, and so look curiously dainty as they balance on the two rails. The train rarely goes faster than 25 mph, but the narrowness of the track means that it rocks sharply from side to side. If they served drinks on the train, you would lose half before you got it to your lips.

From the beginning, an extraordinary *esprit de corps* seemed to motivate everyone who worked for the railway. Five surveying teams, led by one John Hislop, fanned out over the mountains looking for the best route. Hislop himself appeared to be one of those men who can cope without food or sleep, and would go off alone over the peaks with only a few biscuits in his pocket. In the end, by a process of trial and error, the teams found what proved to be the best of all possible routes to the summit. It was fourteen miles from the coast as the crow flies, and the track would need only twenty miles to climb there.

Soapy Smith, of course, opposed the railway, since his whole kingdom was composed of subjects who were stranded in Skagway waiting for money, friends or the means to get their equipment over the pass. As soon as trains began to run, the prospectors would step off the boats and walk straight into their comfortable compartments. Smith did all he could to interfere with the construction. For example, Heney knew that to get the line built he would need to operate a strict ban on alcohol in all the camps.

Smith, seeing a chance for more easy money, set up a drinking and gaming tent near to one. His gang pointed out that they had as much right as anyone to be there. Heney agreed, but gave instructions for a huge rock which overlooked the site to be blasted out of the way. The rock smashed the tent and all the drinks inside it less than a minute after the barman had fled.

However, the railway also provided a focus in Skagway for the opposition to Smith. On 2 July, Samuel Graves, from Chicago, arrived to take over as president of the new White Pass and Yukon Route. According to his own account, in *On The White Pass Pay-roll*, he refused an invitation from Soapy Smith to ride through the town at the head of the 4 July procession. On 6 July, Smith's men robbed a young man of $3000 in gold dust. This shocked and alarmed even the hardened citizens of Skagway, since the young man was the first stampeder to make it back over the pass with his 'poke' of gold since the news of the discovery had reached the world. If it became known that a man could lose all that he had struggled for by passing through the town, Skagway's economy would rapidly collapse. A meeting of vigilantes was held to challenge Smith's rule, and Smith himself, who never lacked physical courage, determined to go down with a Winchester rifle and assert his authority. On the way he met a local businessman, Frank Reid, and in the struggle which followed both men were fatally wounded. Smith died immediately, and all his gang were rounded up and jailed. Reid died some time later, and his grave is marked by a large and imposing monument. Only one mourner attended Smith's funeral, and his remains are acknowledged by nothing but a plain wooden board. Yet it is Soapy who remains Skagway's most famous citizen, as vital and as revered by the tourist industry as Mickey Mouse in Disneyland.

Unimpeded by Smith and his gang, the railway drove forward and upward at impressive speed. The company soon realised that there was no point in shipping labour from the US, since everyone who landed in Skagway would immediately make for the goldfields. However, the town was full of men who had run out of money, luck and hope or else were waiting for something to turn up. They were delighted to have the chance to earn money and get free board and lodging at the same time. By August the railway had a work force of 2000 men. Graves recorded: 'As a general rule, they were immensely superior to ordinary labourers in education and intelligence, but most of them were quite unused to manual labour. However, they soon got hardened to it, and their quick intelligence enabled them to learn rapidly. But the great drawback to them was that by the time they had become useful, their friends, or their money, or whatever they were waiting for, would arrive, and they would resume their journey to the Klondike. In the words of Camp-Foreman Foy, "There was always some a-coming, and some a-going, and some working." Amongst them were lawyers, doctors, artists, college graduates, French chefs, schoolmasters and in short every conceivable sort of occupation – except labourers. Probably no other railway in the world was built by such highly educated men.'

Another problem was that as soon as rumours of another gold strike reached the camps, the work force would up and leave, taking their picks and shovels with them. Soon after construction began, news of a strike in Atlin, British Columbia, reached the White Pass, and in forty-eight hours the work force was reduced by two-thirds. Most of the men came back disconsolate after finding that all the good claims had been staked, a bitter fact of life about most gold strikes, as the first stampeders to reach the Klondike were even then discovering.

The line was blasted from the solid rock through the winter of 1898 and 1899. A 250-foot tunnel, the only one on the line, was literally cut out by hand. Some sections of the line had to be sliced from the side of sheer cliffs, and the labourers hung from ropes dangling over the precipice to do it. There was no gravel for the roadbed in this bleak and rocky terrain, so it had to be hauled up from Skagway. As winter drew in, the temperature sometimes dropped to sixty degrees Fahrenheit below zero. As an engineering feat the first section of the White Pass was remarkable but not unique. To have managed it under such atrocious conditions was, however, almost incredible.

After reaching the summit, the track runs through barren, inhospitable but flatter land to reach Bennett, a lake and town appropriately named after James Gordon Bennett, whose paper, the *New York Herald*, had done much to fan the gold fever. William Randolph Hearst was engaged in a nationwide circulation war at the time, and the sensational articles which appeared in rival newspapers, coupled with the miseries of the Depression, did much to send thousands of young men off on their wretched journey. Bennett was the head of the whole natural navigation system which led to Dawson and the Klondike, and in the winter before the railway was built it was a tent city of around 30,000 men, almost all of them building boats for the equally perilous and fearful trip down-river to the gold. There was almost no aspect of their journey which was not dreadful. To cut the planks which were needed for a boat, two men had to work a whipsaw. This task required tremendous physical exertion combined with remarkable precision, which of course few of the cheechakos could manage. Partnerships which had endured terrible privations on the worst part of the trail

An engine approaches the tunnel on the White Pass and Yukon Route in 1898

were wrecked forever by the boat-building. In the spring of 1898 a church was built on the hill which overlooks Lake Bennett, a rather splendid mock-Gothic affair like a wooden model of half St Pancras. A couple of days before it was due to open the ice broke on the lake so the entire tent city folded up and disappeared north. The church is still there today but no sermon has ever been preached in it.

The line reached Bennett in July 1899, a year to the day after Soapy Smith's death and roughly twelve months from the time construction had begun. The next twenty-seven miles were due to run alongside the lake up to the tiny settlement of Caribou Crossing, which is now known as Carcross. However, since boats could carry the goods, it was decided to press on with the last section to Whitehorse and to build the lakeside line later. This too was an extraordinary achievement, since the land slopes up sharply from the water. The engineers blasted the roadbed and then used the debris to fill in some of the smaller inlets. A work train was crossing one of these when the embankment suddenly gave way, causing that rare occurrence: a train sinking with all hands. No one, however, died. The loyalty to the railway does seem to have been real enough. Graves notes with relish a story about one of the very first tourists ever to ride on the line. He was an American professor of geology. 'Suddenly with great excitement he rushed up to an Irish section-man who was tamping ballast into the new track. "My man, I say, my man, do you know that that broken stone you are using for ballast is a highly mineralised paleozoic formation?"'

The Irishman asked, 'What of it?' and the professor insisted, 'I want you to understand that the ballast is probably worth not less than ten dollars a ton!' Graves adds: 'The Irishman, instead of dropping dead, looked the excited professor calmly in the eye and said, "Well, and I want you to understand, Misther Man, that the bist is none too good for the White Pass". . . and with a snort of indignation he turned to resume tamping of the precious mineral into what, with true White Pass spirit, he regarded as his track.'

The lines met at Carcross in July 1900. Johnny Johns, an Indian trapper and hunting guide (among the many people who have hired his services was Waldemar Graf von Schwein, who was later executed for his part in the plot to kill Hitler. He gave Johns a copy of his book), was two years old at the time, though he reckons to remember the first train arriving. 'I see this monster coming down the tracks, steam coming down both sides, and I figured it was breathing, like people and animals breathe when it's cold. I heard it whistle, and then I really took off.' Johns worked on the railway briefly as a young man; two months of working ten hours a day were enough, particularly in temperatures which could easily reach fifty below. The day the line was finished, the ceremony of the Golden Spike had to be performed. The actual moment came later in the day than had been planned, and most of the participants in the ceremony had been celebrating in the local hotel (which still stands; a battered sign announces a cocktail lounge, and you may eat the best hamburger I can recall in North America). Several dignitaries tried to drive in the final spike, but all of them failed, and in the end the wretchedly mauled object had to be dragged out.

The railway (the Canadians prefer the English word to the American 'railroad') has run continuously ever since, or at any rate run until the winter of 1982 when for the first time in its history it closed down completely until the next summer. Even at the height of the Depression, as the population of the Yukon dwindled, they kept the line open, sometimes waiting for weeks until there was enough freight to pay for the fuel and the crew's wages on a single train. But the railway has always had a switchback economic existence. When it was first built it was extremely profitable, and the high tariffs the White Pass was able to charge for the run from Skagway to Bennett helped to pay for the remaining seventy-odd miles of track to Whitehorse.

Ironically the line reached Bennett almost exactly at the moment the

Gold Rush ended. Gold had been found at Nome in Alaska, and Dawson, the capital of the Klondike, simply began to disappear. Eight thousand people left in a single week, and every steamboat which left the town was jammed with people joining the new stampede. According to Pierre Berton's *Klondike*, the definitive work on the Gold Rush, the dance hall girls complained that their week's takings would not now even pay their laundry bills.

By the time the whole White Pass railway was finished the Gold Rush had become a part of history. However, the fact that the very reason for its existence had vanished did not harm the railway at all. For one thing the big corporations were moving into Dawson and buying up the single claims which had been worked by individual prospectors. Instead of gold pans and home-made sluice boxes they brought in massive industrial plant and this had to be carried by train and steamboat. There is still only one practical principle used for the extraction of gold: this is the fact that it is much heavier than the earth and rock which hold it. All methods of finding gold, whether from a panful of earth or a whole mountain side, involve using water to loosen the soil and stones so that the gold sinks to the bottom.

Through the Depression of the thirties the railway barely survived and might not have lasted the war if it hadn't been for the fact that the Americans feared a Japanese attack on Alaska. To get war materials up from the southern mainland they had to build a highway through Canada and into Alaska, and to do that they had to ship equipment up from the coast. GIs were put in charge of running the railway which they did with formidable efficiency. On one day in 1943, a total of thirty-four trains rolled past the ghost city of Log Cabin, riding on the same elderly tracks laid in such a hurry and in such terrible conditions nearly half a century earlier. Now the railway is facing difficult times again. Foolishly it came to rely too much on only two main cargoes – tourists, and lead-zinc concentrate from the giant Cyrus Anvil mine in the town of Faro. Tourism is booming, with up to 80,000 people riding on the railway each year, or nearly four times the entire population of the Yukon. But the world recession made the mine uneconomic and in the autumn of 1982 it closed down for the winter. There are no tourists in the nine months when it isn't summer, and so the railway had to close down for the winter too. The blow was not only to the 100 or so people laid off, but also to the White Pass's pride. It had never closed down before.

Most people begin their ride on the railway in Skagway. Usually it is a part of an integrated package trip. The tourists arrive from Seattle or

No.73 waits at Skagway station

California by cruise ship, spend the day travelling on the line and pass the night in Whitehorse. Then they may take a coach for the 300 miles to Dawson and the Klondike before heading off into Alaska. When their ship arrives in Skagway there is generally a welcoming party of young people who summer there earning money; they spend most of their time in costumes of the Gold Rush period. In spite of this rather coy appearance Skagway itself is a delightful town. There isn't enough money about to spoil it, and the real reminders of 1898 coexist with the phoney ones. The Red Onion Saloon, for example, contains a 'brothel museum' along with its bars, but it was all a real saloon in 1898, just like the Golden North hotel, and the Skagway Inn. The Pack Train Inn claims to be the oldest establishment in the town, though it did not originally offer its customers 'Video Games, Pinball, Frozen Yoghurt'.

Most of the tourists are elderly and the great majority are American. The tours last longer than the routine holiday fortnight, and so the retired are often the only people who can spare the time. For many it will be their last great package tour, a chance to explore North America's final frontier. Curiously enough they do not look altogether happy, in the way that people on package tours rarely look pleased or relaxed. They interrogate their couriers anxiously, as if terrified that a mistake in the schedule will leave them, or worse, their baggage, behind. I suspect that paradoxically it is the fact that everything is done for them which

White Pass vintage-era parlour cars at Bennett, flanked on the left by the station and restaurant, and on the right by the old wooden church

makes them so dependent, and that this dependence makes them so afraid.

Trains in America tend to roll down the main streets of towns, lumbering and careless like sacred cows in India. The White Pass track continues past the station on to the wharf and on some days the trains stand directly opposite the gangplanks of the cruise ships. The carriages would be familiar to anyone who has ever seen a railroad in a western. Some are more than seventy years old, and no one has had the heart, or the money, to replace them. They have little fenced off verandas at each end, steps leading down to low American platforms, and a chimney in one corner, to carry away the fumes of the acrid stove. That curious horizontally elongated lettering one only sees on American trains reads 'W.P. & Y.R.' along the top of each car, and its name, generally a lake in the area, is spelled out along the side.

Inside the cars the stoves have built up a fug you could eat with a spoon. As you look through the windows it seems barely possible that we can get out of Skagway; the town is bounded on one side by sea and on the other three by precipitous mountains. A hint of the exertions to come is furnished by the locomotives: as many as six engines may be linked together to start the climb. The train lumbers slowly through the town, turns left and heads directly at the mountains. After two miles it passes the Gold Rush Cemetery where Soapy Smith and Frank Reid, the man who killed him, are both buried. Not surprisingly it is Smith's grave which draws the tourists, and one anonymous admirer sent $50 a year, shortly after Smith's death, for its upkeep. Reid's marble slab says, 'He gave his life for the honor of Skagway', though in matters of honour the town was closer to being a strumpet than a maiden. An early tourist promoter called Martin Itjen painted a large rock gold and called it the 'Largest Gold Nugget in the World'. Tourism began almost as soon as the Gold Rush ended; a newspaper advert promoted the charms of this graveyard and the remains of 'Soapy Smith, the desperado who ruled Skagway in the early days'. That was in 1910, just twelve years after Smith met his end.

Soon the train begins the spectacular, creaking climb towards the summit. The narrowness of the track and the shakiness of the carriages increases the sense of vertigo most passengers feel now. At Rocky Point, seven miles out of Skagway, you can make out the town and the wharf, the whole overhung by the Harding Glacier. Snow and ice are always visible from Skagway even through the summer. Then a mile and a half later is one of those strange signs you sometimes see from trains (there was an advert saying 'Uncle Joe's Mintballs Leave You All Aglow' visible from the Glasgow line near Wigan). This one reads 'On To Alaska With Buchanan'. The mysterious giant letters painted on the far side of the canyon do not, however, refer to some hearty nineteenth-century explorer, but to a boys' tour group from Cleveland which somehow continued to paint their message onto rock in the thirties.

One of the first fatal accidents on the line is marked at Black Cross Rock, ten miles out of town, where in August 1898 two men were buried by a 100-ton granite slab loosened during blasting. Thirty people died in constructing the railway. A mile later are the splendid Bridal Veil Falls, water pouring from the glacier on Mount Cleveland. Now and again you glimpse a trail, a moss-covered track which may have been used by the original stampeders, or is still used today by walkers. Convenient leaflets warn how to behave in the presence of bears. Don't run away; the beast may panic and pursue you. Don't ever feed them or they may associate humans with sustenance and start to eat people as a substitute for buns.

If you are fortunate you may be hauled by the last steam locomotive working on the line. Engine 73 (American railroads number their locomotives roughly in order of acquisition. Since 'Engine 1047' would not have quite the same romantic ring, British Rail names its locos after newspapers, politicians and branded malt whiskies) was built at the Baldwin Locomotive Works in Philadelphia. It was one of a series which had been designed specially for the railway, and the first of this '70 Class' were built in 1938. For those interested in the technical details, they had a Mikado type 2–8–2 wheel arrangement, a two-wheeled pony truck, four sets of

An overhanging cliff in Skagway River valley dwarfs 2–8–0 No. 68 on the White Pass line

driving wheels, and an inside frame, unlike many engines built specifically for narrow gauges. The steam was 'superheated', which meant that it was passed through the pipe twice in order to dry it and heat it up even more before it reached the piston cylinders.

Numbers 72 and 73 came after the war, when the company needed new engines to haul the increasing ore traffic. The White Pass were so pleased with their performance that they actually requested half a dozen more steam engines at a time when railroads all over the world were switching to diesel and electrics. Baldwin's refused, saying they would need a minimum order of ten, and reluctantly the railway began to buy diesels from General Electric. What everyone assumed would be the last steam trip of all ran in 1964. Engine 73 was retired to Bennett as a museum piece until the eighties, when the railway spent a year restoring it. Now a gleaming black, with charcoal grey smoke pouring from its funnel, the train makes eight or so excursions a year. It's odd how you forget what you have forgotten about steam; the sharp catch of the smoke at the back of the throat, the rich burnt smell, the rhythm of the engine which feels and sounds like a beast of burden, painfully forcing itself up the hills rather than gliding with the dull effortlessness of a diesel.

Frequently Engine 73 is driven by J.D. True, an American driver who lives in Skagway and is the doyen of the 'hogheads'. This was originally an abusive term for engineers who mismanaged the throttle and burned too much fuel. Like 'hack' for journalist, the word has now become almost a badge of pride on the railway.

True has been in some of the most spectacular crashes on the line. 'In 1965 I went down the Canyon, just the other side of Eight Mile, looking across at the US customs post. When they first built the railroad there was a trestle there, but later they built a cement retaining wall, using river gravel for fill. Since 1908, that wall was under constant pressure. We came round the corner and we could see the track hanging out there, and there was nothing under it.' The line had become as useless as two pieces of string slung across the void. True and the others in the cab were trapped and their locomotive fell for 250 feet, though the engine behind it crashed 1000 feet and wasn't recovered from the gorge for more than a year. True smashed his pelvis, but when the loco came back from repair in Calgary, he was the first back inside the cab.

He does seem to attract trouble. When we were in Skagway the local paper carried news of True's latest crash on its front page. Fifteen miles out of Skagway, Engine 73 had hit a rockslide. 'From the time we hit until we stopped wasn't a great distance, but we didn't know whether the engine

Engine 73 is inspected in Glacier Gorge

was going to stay upright or not. It was a pretty good feeling when it finally stopped. Those big boulders, looked to me like fifteen or twenty of them, looked as big as Volkswagen Beetles. Some had bounced and gone over into the canyon. The track looked like pretzels.' One tourist said she thought it had been a deliberate part of the ride, as on a fake railway it might have been. But the White Pass is real, immediately real. As Steve Hites, the railway's ceaselessly and infectiously enthusiastic 'Passenger Services Representative', says: 'That's real wildlife out there. Those aren't mechanical bears that go "rowrr" when you punch a button at the side of the track and the train goes by.'

At the fifteen-mile post the passengers see the most astonishing sight on the line. The railway calls it 'flying by train'. To gain height, the line climbs with gradients of up to four per cent along the sheer rock faces of a massive V-shaped gorge. From inside the cars you can see nothing except the trees and rocks hundreds of feet below. Passengers brace themselves perilously against the spindly rails at the end of each car, simultaneously holding their cameras tight, trying to focus them and jamming their knees against the metalwork. The train crosses Glacier Gorge by trestle, then buries itself into the one tunnel built on the route to the summit.

After seventeen miles, the train, by now heaving and panting with the effort, reaches Inspiration Point, where there is an astonishing view down to Skagway and the sea. There is a plaque here devoted to the memory of

Engine 73 crossing the trestle bridge over Glacier Gorge

the 3000 pack animals which died during the 1898 stampede. Many finished their wretched, burdened lives in Dead Horse Gulch, now a charnel house of white bones. Their half-crazed owners drove them off the cliff as soon as they saw that there was no more strength left in them. The frightening thing was that the stampeders were not especially harsh or cruel men; for the most part they were extremely ordinary folk, grocers' assistants, farm hands, bank clerks. What they had come to share was a delirium about gold which transcended and destroyed their normal emotions and judgements. Some of the hardest cruelties were committed by men who would not have raised a hand against an animal at home.

At twenty miles, the White Pass summit marks the border between Canada and the United States. This is the spot where the Mounties checked each stampeder to make sure they had the obligatory year's worth of supplies and did not carry any side-arms. There are no customs or immigration posts

Double-headed mixed train crosses Dead Horse Gulch viaduct in 1946

here, just two flags to mark the crossing. The real formalities are observed further along the highway at what must be one of the quietest immigration offices in the world. Passengers who arrive in Skagway have their passports stamped by the most charming immigration officer I've ever met; for those used to New York, where they tend to take the view that you are a drug-ridden illegal immigrant unless you can prove otherwise, the experience is somewhat disconcerting.

Fraser is the tiny settlement, high on the Pass, which serves as the customs and immigration post for Canada. Here one or two of the more earnest travellers get off the train to begin hiking. It must be an eerie occasion for them watching the train leave, its whistle blowing sadly in the wind, for there is nothing at all here, no shops and scarcely any people. Fraser was the headquarters of the snow plough team which was used to keep the line open in the very worst conditions. These old ploughs had at the front a set

White Pass rotary unit – 18 miles from Skagway

of huge rotating knives, a little like a gigantic food processor, and were pushed along the track by the regular engines. The blades sliced through the snow and hurled it left or right of the track, according to the direction of the nearest chasm.

Considering that they were built even before 1898, when the railway began, these ploughs were astonishingly effective, and stayed in service until the 1950s when they were replaced by bulldozers. They could move no faster than walking speed – often much slower – and were not always adequate when the snow was really deep. If it reached higher than twelve feet, men had to dig away with shovels until the level was low enough for the plough to cope. Very rarely the weather was so bad that the wheels of the engine froze to the track, and then all movement became impossible. Sometimes the crews had to be on duty for days at a stretch in order to keep the lines clear. During one tremendous storm in 1900, a train pushing a rotary plough left Skagway on 7 March, and reached Bennett, forty miles away, on 11 March. The crew worked for 105 hours, of which 90 hours was continuous and without sleep. The passengers did something which must be almost unique in railway history: they joined together on the train to write and present a testimonial to the men who had got them through.

Graves provides a vivid description of the perils of snow clearance: 'The first snow-bank is soon reached and the rotary started. As soon as it is running steadily its engineer gives the signal to the snorting monsters behind and they commence to force him relentlessly into the hidden dangers of the snow-bank. But a rotary engineer is not supposed to worry about hidden dangers – he confines himself to the situation in hand, regulating the speed of his revolving knives and the speed at which he is being pushed into the snow according to the exigencies of the moment. Nervous passengers prefer not to look down into the canyons below. But the engineer must not waste time speculating about what would happen if there were a rail loose under the snow-bank into which the three monsters behind are blindly forcing him forward . . . nor is it of the slightest use speculating about the result should the snow on the mountain above begin to slide.

'One's ears are deafened by the noise of the monsters snorting behind and by the roar of snow as it is whirled through and out of the hood. In the midst of this bewildering din stands the rotary engineer with his hand on the throttle and his eyes all round him, ready for anything, but expecting nothing. Clearly it is no place for a weakling. Then perhaps the water runs short, and your oil cups freeze, and your feet freeze, and you have been forty-eight hours on your legs, and the "worst is yet to come". But you must stick to it like a bulldog and get the train through. And you do – if you are a White Pass man.'

Poorer labour relations, and a management which has not responded to modern conditions as skilfully as it might, have reduced this extraordinary spirit among the employees, but have not extinguished it. You still find traces of a powerful emotional commitment to the line which you do not encounter very often elsewhere.

The next place on the route is, if 'place' is not too strong a word, the town of Log Cabin. This now consists of a grand total of two buildings, both around the size of potting sheds: downtown Log Cabin and suburban Log Cabin. Once there was another tent city here, used by the stampeders trekking towards the lake. Now it is two unoccupied section houses for the railway. Here the line crosses the Skagway to Whitehorse highway, a dusty road which is closed in winter for obvious reasons, and on which you hope very much not to meet a truck coming in the opposite direction. Happily the existence of the railway as a means of hauling freight makes this unlikely. People in Whitehorse are slightly puzzled about the existence of the road at all, since goods and tourists all go by train. 'I guess it's useful if we want to go to Alaska for a game of baseball, or maybe if we just want to visit Skagway and bask in the rain,' one Whitehorse inhabitant told us.

At Log Cabin we were picked up by a 'motor car', a little orange workshop on wheels which the railway uses to reach parts of the line in need of repair. It's not exactly comfy, but it is spectacular, a little like crossing the

Rockies on a milk float. At the time of year we were there the view is unimaginably beautiful; the trees are a shimmering, translucent gold, their pale colour heightened by the low autumnal sun. Banks of ever-greens slice into the yellow, and there are occasional vivid splashes of red. The lakes are a piercing blue at the middle of the day, then become a more sullen grey as dusk begins to gather. The clouds descend near to the mountains, so that the sky, while it spreads for seemingly hundreds of miles, feels peculiarly close, as if you could reach up and touch it. The wind rushes through the trees, the telegraph lines begin to hum, leaving the impression that a ghostly string quintet might be playing far away.

A few miles further on, the train begins to roll through 'Thirty-four flats', a name which refers to nothing more romantic than the fact that the plains are thirty-four miles from Skagway. You might, if you are lucky, see a caribou or a moose here, though this does not happen often, since the animals prefer to walk out in the evening, after the train has gone by.

Moose is an important part of the Yukon's life and economy. White people may take out a licence which permits them to shoot one each season and men will go out hunting for several weekends at a stretch to find their one beast. Some are lazy and blast away from inside their cars. But your true hunter stalks the moose with wiles and cunning, being prepared to wait in severe discomfort for hours or days to find it. Experts can blow 'moose calls' which sound, slightly, like the female moose. They hope that a lustful male will hear and come charging across the wilderness into range of their rifles. It quite often works, though the signal might just as easily be heard by a grizzly bear who, on arrival, will express his anger and disappointment in tangible fashion. Nor does shooting always work. 'You can hit a grizzly, then he'll slap the shit out of you before going off to die a few miles away,' one huntsman told us.

A moose has around 1000 pounds of edible meat on its carcase. The Yukon in winter serves as its own deep freeze, and so for some families moose is the only meat they eat for months. Luckily the taste is good, a little like gamy beef. It can also be cooked in several dozen different ways (the *Yukon Cookbook* lists fifty-five different recipes including Moose Shish Kebabs, Moose Tripe Sausage, Boiled Moose Nose and something called *Paupiettes de Moose Biscoise*). By the end of winter this must get somewhat wearying; there ought to be an old Yukon adage: 'no moose is good moose.'

Forty miles north of Skagway the train rolls into Bennett. This city which for one winter had 30,000 inhabitants is now nothing but a feeding halt for the railway. The passengers descend, glad to get their feet on the solid wooden boards of the station platform, and queue politely for their meal. They march in to long communal tables, each already stocked with the day's lunch: potatoes, beans of an uncompromising nature, and great hot bowls of stew. The railway would like its passengers to think, though it doesn't actually pretend, that this is made from moose. Sometimes it is, but more often it is beef. It's cheaper to ship this from Chicago than to send employees out to hunt the local fauna. There are vacuum flasks filled with coffee, and the passengers scoff it all eagerly. The rigours of the journey and the keen mountain air sharpen the appetite well. Next door most of the railwaymen who work this stretch of line have already eaten, and from an extensive menu. The old-timers might have survived on pemmican and sourdough bread, but a daily diet of stew and beans would not persuade many people to stay working in this inhospitable place. Steve Hites, if he is on the journey, moves around the tables explaining what happened in Bennett more than eighty years ago; sometimes his own enthusiasm communicates itself to the tourists, but as often as not they seem vague and perplexed. They are as likely to spend their time asking exactly how they will know the train is due to depart as they will inquiring about the past. Their subliminal terror of being left behind makes it hard for them to enjoy the ride as much as they might.

After lunch the braver spirits set off for the old wooden church and the astonishing view down towards the White Pass. Now and again a hiker appears at the end of one of the trails which led to Bennett before the railway was built. The walk from Skagway or Dyea can be managed in two or a more comfortable three days, and they ride the train back to the sea.

Many of the tourists finish their trip here, and take the next train south. There are a few more locals on the ride north towards Whitehorse; calmer, more laconic people, given to accepting the extremes of climate and environment without letting anything excite them unduly. The engines fuss around attaching themselves to the correct line of cars, their drivers blow whistles to draw the stragglers back down from the hills, and Hites reassures another dozen people that they are on the right train. The crews change here: Americans living in Skagway operate the engines as far as Bennett, where Canadians who live in Whitehorse take over.

Our train begins the twenty-seven-mile-long ride by the shores of Lake Bennett. In bad weather, Bennett looks more like an inland sea, with great grey swells and black clouds seeming to skim across its surface. At the far end of the lake is the only real settlement anywhere along the line apart from its two terminals. This is the town of Caribou Crossing, or Carcross. By the time we reached there I had developed a nasty headache due only in part to the thick fug in the carriage. This was produced by both the stove and by the quantities of high-fibre beans eaten by my fellow passengers. I explained the problem to the conductor who assured me that I could go to Matthew Watson's General Store, Carcross, to buy some aspirin. 'I'll hold the train for you,' he beamed. It's the kind of railway where you can ask that kind of favour.

Next to the store is the Caribou Hotel, proudly advertising its 'cocktail lounge'. The hotel is the town's social centre, serving the customers home cooking and apparently endless coffee. You could spend a day there happily watching the whole life of a sub-Arctic community pass in miniature: Indian trappers, truckers, the local Mountie, fishermen and housewives.

Johnny Johns, the Indian guide, lives here, and told us why he likes it. 'It's the wide open spaces. There's no fences here. In Whitehorse,' he said with distaste, 'you have to tie up your dog.' In this part of the world that counts as uncomfortable restriction. Johns still does a lot of hunting here, sometimes vanishing for several days at a time. 'You can hunt coyote, wolf, wolverine, mink, beaver and lynx. Gopher tastes good. You roast them until they're golden brown. It tastes a bit like chicken but I prefer gopher. You skewer them through the necks and roast 'em, like a kebab. Whites eat red squirrel, but I don't like them, there's no flavour to them.'

The train chugs off again winding across the milder, more tractable landscape. We pass Robinson, one of the scores of ghost towns which dot the countryside here. There are now more ghost towns than living settlements in the Yukon. Most of them are small clutches of dark log cabins with dank earth floors. At sunrise and sunset the wood glows bronze. Sometimes a town will be only half deserted; next to the empty houses you may see a wooden shack with ragged curtains and smoke rising from the chimney. For some reason people here never seem to ditch their old cars, so every small settlement will be flanked by the rusting hulks of pick-up vans. There are sprucer weekend cabins too. There are so many lakes here, so many forests and nameless mountains, that almost every inhabitant of Whitehorse could have his own idyllically situated cabin out of sight of all his neighbours. At least this used to be the case; at the end of a long and bruising campaign, the native Indians have won their claim to most of the Yukon's land so that in some of the wildest and least populated areas, building sites are as hard to find as in Manhattan. Anyone must have sympathy with the Indians cursorily robbed of their lands, yet it seems strange that this huge territory – bigger than the British Isles, West Germany and Belgium combined – should be criss-crossed with invisible lines of ownership.

Finally we run into Whitehorse, passing the Rapids on the way. Here was the greatest peril on the whole of the river route to the goldfields. When the stampeders reached here from Bennett, 150 boats were destroyed and five men drowned in the first few days. Most lost everything they had, the appalling labours of the winter lost in a few seconds on the furious water. After these disasters, the next gold hunters decided not to chance the rapids, and a traffic jam of several thousand boats blocked the canyon upstream. The chaos was sorted out by the Mounties, in particular Sam Steele, who remains a legendary figure in the Yukon. Steele was in the habit of making up the law as he went along, and so saved hundreds of lives during the stampede. He announced that unfit people would have to walk the five miles along the bank by the rapids, and that no boat would be allowed to attempt the trip unless it was safely built and competently steered. He also decreed hundred-dollar fines for anyone who disobeyed. As a result the wreckage almost stopped. It is an interesting clue to why the Canadian frontier has never had the mystique of the American West; it was actually too well administered. Thanks to the Mounties, the Gold Rush towns were literally no more lawless than Little Rissington, Glos. This made life a lot easier for the inhabitants but was hardly the stuff of movie legend.

There is scant serious crime in Whitehorse today, and most of what there is occurs because of alcohol. Winter can be terribly depressing; the local description for this is 'cabin fever', a state of psychological dejection brought on by the sheer difficulty of getting out of the house and the fact that there is no good reason for going outside in the first place.

Some people get drunk, others get miserable, and a tiny handful go berserk, goaded to terrible violence because their partner picks his teeth or whistles annoyingly. I spoke to one young woman who said there was a kind of urban cabin fever which people in the town suffered: 'It is so bloody cold and dark, you think "there's a whole world out there, and here are we sitting in the dark." You end up beating your wife or going to Mexico. It's like a kind of human hibernation.' In early spring, when the days have begun to get a little longer and there is more than four hours of murky daylight, they hold the Sourdough Rendezvous, a week-long festival of games, sports and drinking at which the whole town, indeed the whole Yukon Territory, celebrates the fact that somewhere, out there, the good weather and the endless daylight might be waiting.

There is also the consolation of friendship. It's a classless sort of society; it has to be when you have a tiny population living on the edge of survival. The Yukon now has a measure of self-government and its own legislature (Conservative at the moment; the almost exclusively Indian settlement of Old Crow near the Arctic Ocean must contain the most northerly Tories in the world). The Cabinet includes an ice-rink attendant, a housewife, and an unemployed Indian. This sense of self-reliance can make the place inward-looking. They use the term 'outside' to mean everywhere south of the sixtieth parallel, which means everywhere in North America except the Yukon, Alaska and the Northern Territories. A bumper sticker proclaims: 'Who gives a damn how they do things outside?'

The Yukon River runs, swift and ice-cold, at the edge of the town. Along the banks are the great empty flat-bed trucks which belong to the railway. In autumn the temperature can reach an agreeable sixty or seventy degrees, but at night it is freezing, and the first warmth of the day brings the steam smoking up off the river. Like the people who live here the railway is a survivor, sometimes apparently destroyed by the weather or the economy but somehow always bouncing back. They are mocking and self-deprecating about the Yukon here – a tee-shirt in a tourist shop says: 'Eat drink and be merry, for tomorrow you may be in Whitehorse', but this is a bluff; they are fiercely proud of the place and just as proud of their own ability to live here and be happy. I liked and admired them, and their railway. As so many people promised me, I felt drawn back there. Robert Service called one of his best-known verses 'The Spell of the Yukon' and in its rushing energy he caught some of the feel:

> The winter! The brightness that blinds you,
> The white land locked tight as a drum,
> The cold fear that follows and finds you,
> The silence that bludgeons you dumb.
> The snows that are older than history,
> The woods where the weird shadows slant;
> The stillness, the moonlight, the mystery,
> I've bade 'em goodbye – but I can't.

> There's gold, and it's haunting and haunting,
> It's luring me on as of old;
> Yet it isn't the gold that I'm wanting,
> So much as just finding the gold.
> It's the great, big, broad land 'way up yonder,
> It's the forests where silence has lease,
> It's the beauty that thrills me with wonder,
> It's the stillness that fills me with peace.

THE PHILIPPINES
The Dragons of Sugar Island
COLIN GARRATT

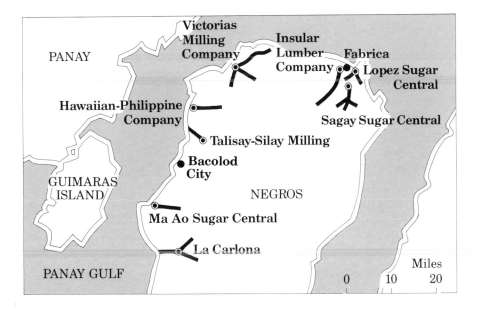

We weren't really interested in overseas railways before the 1960s. The diversity of Britain's railway network with its one and a half centuries of history was more than sufficient for most students. Foreign locomotives were generally regarded as ugly and those from America had a reputation for being cheaply constructed. However, by 1965 it became evident that steam traction in the land of its birth was doomed, as were large sections of the railway network. Only ten years previously, Britain had operated almost 30,000 steam locomotives embracing hundreds of different types and few people anticipated their extinction. But technological advances during the 1960s were so rapid that in 1968 the end came and British Railways ran their last steam train; millions of people openly expressed their grief. Letters to the national press claimed that Britain would never be the same again, and a handful of people emigrated to lands where steam traction reigned supreme. Others turned to preservation and raised funds to purchase locomotives and abandoned branch lines. The results of such efforts are well known today with such popular attractions as the Bluebell Railway, the Festiniog and dozens of others. Britain now leads the world in railway preservation – some recompense for the mother country having partly abandoned her great railway heritage. Magnificent as these museum lines are, they lack the atmosphere of the authentic; they are, in effect, technological zoos; a steam locomotive on a museum line is like a wild beast in captivity. The experience is secondhand and much of the subject's inherent magic dissipated.

The disappearance of steam in Britain led to a renaissance in railway enthusiasm, and attention became focused upon the global scene in an effort to compensate for what had been lost at home. For me, 1968 was a watershed, as having watched and studied trains for almost twenty years, I realised what a significant role the steam locomotive had played in the development of the industrial world. It was evident that, following Britain's lead, other countries would declare against steam, and I felt that documentation on a global scale needed to be made. Thus the following year I abandoned a promising commercial career with the avowed intention of recording upon film and in words the last steam locomotives of the world.

Having taken this step, I began a vast research project to ascertain the whereabouts of the surviving locomotives, and it was during this period that I came across a picture of an incredible American-styled Mallet working on the Philippine island of Negros. My imagination was completely captured by this engine as it was more akin to one of Emmett's fantastic creations than a real locomotive. Yet for all its hybridised decrepitude, it personified the romantic aura of the racy balloon-stacked engines which once roared across the plains of the old Wild West.

If the big Mallet was anything to go by, there could be other engines of equally incredible appearance and historical significance. I intensified my researches and discovered that the island had some Shays – a particularly exotic form of locomotive which was on the verge of extinction.

The Shays and Mallet worked for a company known as the Insular Lumber Company (ILCo.), based at Fabrica in the northern part of the island. The engines consumed the mahogany of the forests and sent palls of fire into the air when working. So inspiring were these locomotives, that I dreamed of capturing on film a Shay and the Mallet, at the dead of night, standing side by side and bathed in fire. Had I been a painter, I could have easily manifested such a vision, but as a photographer I had physically to go there and grapple with whatever problems were involved.

Having made plans for an expedition, I wrote to ILCo. asking them to confirm that their railway would be operating – my fear being that the system may have closed and the engines been cut up by a local scrap merchant. Less than a fortnight before I planned to go, an answer arrived; 'Our Mallet and Shay locomotives will be operating at the time of your proposed visit and we shall be pleased to welcome you to Fabrica.'

Ten days later, I boarded the evening flight from Manila to Bacolod, the capital of Negros. The journey was a romantic one for I had a thrilling mission on an exotic tropical island. I was – I had been told in Manila – going to a Paradise Island where 'the people are charming in disposition, beautiful in appearance and the most hospitable on earth'. Furthermore, it was said that Bacolod is called the city of smiles. The sight of a guard armed with a machine gun standing at the rear of the plane did something to dispel my illusions, but the flight proved uneventful and one hour later we arrived at Bacolod and I stepped down into a dream.

Bacolod clearly indicates its American past as the Philippines, following over 400 years of Spanish rule, came under American administration from 1898 until independence in 1946. The city was built from sugar profits in the 1920s and has a distinctly Midwest atmosphere. The brightly coloured jeep which conveyed me to the Sea Breeze Hotel was festooned with slogans and garish transfer pictures, which personified the vigorous outgoing nature of an exciting people, whose beautiful features represent a fusion of Latin and Polynesian blood. American disco music howled from cracked speakers in roadside cafés, and the city had an optimistic atmosphere which hinted at a thriving commercial base.

The journey up to Fabrica took several hours on wet crowded roads and it was dark when I arrived. Upon reporting to ILCo's operations office, I was told that the general manager had gone up to Base Camp at Minapasuk and would not return until tomorrow. I asked about the Mallet and Conrado Gabriel, the operations superintendent, said, 'You mean No.7, she's on her way down from Minapasuk with a loaded train – she will be here in about three hours.' A three-hour wait in the steadily falling rain was nothing compared with the years I had waited to see this engine.

Conrado took me to a nearby shanty-type coffee stall where local coffee boiling in a tub was strained through sacking before being poured into table glasses. These coffee houses, though spartan, have a homely atmosphere and provide a gathering point for the local people. We sat down and inevitably I was bombarded with questions as to my purpose in visiting Fabrica. Conrado listened intently. 'No.7's a strange one,' he said shaking his head. 'She's a man killer. More people have died through that engine than I care to mention; some say she's haunted.'

Conrado and his friends were intrigued by my travelling halfway round the world to see their railway, and I was able to extract some useful information from them. The Mallet was the principal mainline engine being employed to carry logs from Base Camp up in the hills down to Fabrica where the company's sawmills were situated. The Shays were used primarily for operations around Fabrica although one, usually No.12, remained up at Base Camp to shunt the sidings and make up the loaded rakes for the Mallet. Conrado confirmed that No.7 was built by Baldwins in Philadelphia in 1925 to a gauge of three feet six inches and that she was a genuine four-cylinder Compound in accordance with classic American traditions. 'It is my belief,' he continued, 'that she came second-hand from neighbouring Cebu Island during the last war – I began here in 1946 and she was mainline engine then. However, there is a retired ILCo. employee living here in Fabrica, who says he remembers No.7 arriving new during the 1920s; in truth I don't think anyone knows for certain.

'Everything here is run down and semi-derelict,' Conrado said. 'The woods are almost cut out and every month come fresh rumours of closure. Our track is extremely dangerous; no maintenance is done and no money spent on it. On every trip No.7 derails, but since so few logs are now conveyed – they only have a load for her every twenty-four hours – there is usually sufficient time for several rerailings to be carried out, so naturally the company will not invest in track or locomotives.

'These engines are ghosts which refuse to die,' Conrado continued. 'Of course our men can keep them going by ingeniously making parts at our workshop here in Fabrica, but only a steam locomotive would survive under such primitive working conditions. As the boilers get weaker, we have to reduce the steam pressure. When I came here, No.7 could haul thirty-two thirty-ton log cars, but since we reduced her working pressure from 280 pounds per square inch to 220 pounds, she has difficulty in bringing down sixteen! But as I say, the mountain stands are almost cut out, so no one cares. She's a dangerous engine – you keep well away from her.'

I felt curiously at home with my new companions; they were down-to-earth people who worked hard for meagre returns, but they had warm personalities and the hours passed amicably. Suddenly a bell rang out in the control room across the road; Conrado rose to his feet and hurried over to answer it. He emerged minutes later and, standing outlined against the light streaming through the doorway, called, 'No.7's within two kilometres.'

I felt a surging thrill as the crossing gates over the Bacolod-Sagay road rattled down and a distant whistle rang out like a cold shiver. The darkness became filled with the most hideous sounds ever emitted from a locomotive as, with hollow rasps from her uneven exhaust, the enormous mahogany-

Hawaiian-Philippine's Dragon No. 7 with stove-pipe chimney

burning Mallet – twice as large as I had imagined – eased herself tender first over the crossing. I was spellbound by the disjointed and freakish conglomeration of locomotion; she was unique. With mahogany sparks curling off her smokestack and rasping steam from all cylinders, she clanked past, her trainload of log cars piled high with trunks eerily gliding after her into the gloom.

'You've seen nothing yet,' Conrado said, motioning me towards a company jeep, and we drove off along a muddy road in pursuit of the train. 'We will just be in time to see No. 7 working above the sawmills log pan,' he called. Eventually the road opened out into the works area, and I noticed that the train had stopped on a ledge high above a huge artificial lake. The logs were to be pushed mechanically from the wagons, and allowed to crash violently down a slope into the water below. From here a conveyor took them to the sawmill – the logs being easier to process when wet.

From the opposite side of the lake, I watched No. 7 ease a log car into position, and after grappling with it for a few seconds, the pusher dislodged an enormous trunk and sent it thundering down into the pan. The ground shook under the impetus and when the log finally hit the lake it sent a terrific spray of water some forty feet skywards. With three trunks sent down in rapid succession, the Mallet drew her wagons forward emitting grotesque sounds from her four leaking cylinders, all of which had their valves out of alignment. Like an anguished creature she moved forward, her acrid silhouette – back-lit by sodium lights from the mill – was seen to be ever changing in ghostly patterns amid fire and swirling steam. After all logs had been ejected, she pushed the cars out of the mill, every slip of a wheel obscuring her in steam and showers of crimson sparks.

No.7 was one of the last surviving remnants of the Mallet lineage which found its ultimate flowering in North America, with the biggest steam locomotives of all time – the Union Pacific's 4–8–8–4 *Big Boys* which weighed 550 tons. The Mallet was created a century ago in 1884, when a Frenchman named Anatole Mallet produced a semi-articulated tank engine with the main frame split into two units: the rear one rigid, the leading one articulated. Mallet's engine was a four-cylinder compound and the two high-pressure cylinders drove the rear fixed unit. The exhaust steam then passed to the low-pressure cylinders which drove the front unit. The Mallet became the most important articulated steam type and appeared in count-less manifestations ranging from small industrial locomotives to fully fledged mainliners. Traditionally, the Mallet was a compound, although many later designs were simples in which steam was fed direct from the boiler to all four cylinders. An estimated 5000 locomotives were built to the Mallet principle.

In purely historical terms Fabrica was more significant for having one of the world's last colonies of Shays, and shortly after the Mallet had taken the empties back to the sidings, Lima Shay No.10, a three-cylinder B type, began tripping loads of planks from the sawmill up to the planing mill. The engine's appearance was quite hideous; her massive spark-arresting chimney included a cut-down oil drum, whilst the improvised buffer beam and running plates were made from baulks of wood! Here was blissful decrepitude. The noise issuing from No.10 was quite fearsome as, shuffling along at a crawl, she ground and crashed her gears over the rickety tracks, flinging masses of flaming mahogany thirty yards from the tracksides.

The Shay was the traditional lumber engine of the American Pacific North-West and the brainchild of a backwoods logging engineer named Ephraim Shay. The type was adopted by Lima of Ohio, who took a patent on the design. The Shay combines good articulation with an efficient transmission of power to move the train. To fulfil these requirements, Shays are mounted flexibly on four-wheeled bogies known as trucks; many are of the two-truck variety in which the leading truck is set beneath the smokebox and the rear one behind the cab. A two-truck Shay is designated B type, a three-truck C type and a four-truck D type. The cylinders – usually two or three in number – are situated alongside each other in a vertical position just ahead of the cab on the engine's right-hand side.

These cylinders drive a horizontal crankshaft running the entire length of the engine, the drive being applied by pinions slotting into bevelled gears on the truck wheels. The crankshaft is made flexible by incorporating universal joints placed at intervals throughout its length. The gearing ratio applied to the small wheels gives an even turning movement, and so reduces slipping. Such transmission is achieved at the cost of speed and fifteen to twenty mph may be regarded as the Shay's upper limit, but for logging operations reliability and pugnacity are of the essence, rather than speed of transit.

Logging lines are, by definition, light in construction, heavily graded and tightly curved. The tracks are often poorly maintained and not infrequently engulfed in mud. No conventional engine would perform under such extreme conditions.

The experiences of that first night heightened my determination to photograph a Shay and Mallet bathed in fire, and upon explaining this to Conrado, he confirmed that such a picture was possible at Minapasuk. He suggested that I spend the night in the company's guest house and discuss a visit to Base Camp with the Operations Manager, Sr Simplicio Moreno, the following morning. I was lulled to sleep that night by the cacophony of sounds issuing from the Shays in the nearby works.

Shortly after 6.00 a.m., Conrado came to the guest house along with Sr Moreno who invited me to spend several days at his house up at Base Camp. We made the twenty-one-mile journey to Minapasuk by diesel trolley; the track condition was unbelievably bad, and it was difficult to imagine how the trains ever stayed on the line. The system was obviously near to closure and I realised that I was witnessing the end of an era, for already ILCo. – as a classic American-styled logging railway – had a legendary status.

Minapasuk was an isolated shanty town which served the logging community. The logs were trucked in from the distant hills and the marshalling was done by Shay No.12, a huge three-cylinder C type engine, ostensibly built by Lima in 1907. Moreno explained that Mallet No.7 came for the loads once every twenty-four hours, but the timing was irregular because of derailments. She was however expected that night, and it was agreed that we should go down to the exchange sidings when the train arrived. But before the day was over, the sky began to look black and ominous; Moreno confirmed that a typhoon was in the area and warned of bad weather for several days ahead.

The rain had begun in earnest when a midnight telephone call from the yard foreman advised us that the train had arrived. Moreno produced an enormous umbrella and, armed with two torches, we made our way down the hillside. The railway was rapidly turning into a quagmire and mud rose above our ankles. In appalling discomfort we struggled on until there appeared through the darkness ahead a column of fire rising some fifty feet into the air. Another column suddenly erupted alongside as the two engines shunted in the siding. In many years of railway experiences, seldom had I witnessed anything so beautiful. Here in the mountains of this remote island two survivors from dynasties long since forgotten played out their final moments. I felt like a naturalist approaching a cave of dinosaurs.

The heady excitement I felt was tempered by the rain which had now become torrential. Photography that night was out of the question; the two of us were soaked to the skin, and in deference to Moreno, I suggested that we return to the house. I was to remain indoors for the following two days until the typhoon passed, and only on the evening of the second day was it practical for me to venture outside.

Once the rain stopped the temperature and humidity rose dramatically and shrouds of steam issued from the jungle around. The railway lines had completely disappeared beneath the mud, and the green-clad mountains were bathed in a twilight mist. Up at the loading area logs were piled high in a tangled mass which contrasted starkly with the lifting gear. Standing in a quagmire, I watched the twilight deepen and listened to the melodious whistle cry of Shay No.12 on her way up from Maaslud. A chattering flurry from her pounding cylinders finally broke the silence as she crossed the Himog An river bridge, and soon her bizarre shape emerged through the mists beneath a swirl of fire.

By sheer good fortune, the Mallet was due to come up again later that evening and, having collected my photographic equipment, I climbed aboard No.12's footplate intending to spend some hours with the crew and be on location at the exchange point in Maaslud sidings. As we shunted through the leafy groves, spray from the wet palm fronds cascaded into the cab providing refreshing relief from the footplate's clammy heat.

By midnight, Shay No.12 was simmering quietly at Maaslud waiting for the Mallet; news had already come through that she had derailed and would be late. My only fear was that the train would arrive after dawn, which broke at around 4.30. Moreno joined us, bringing a welcome flask of coffee. He insisted upon staying with me despite the distinct possibility of a second derailment delaying the train until the following day. By 2.00 a.m. my nerves were becoming strained; if I failed this time it could be many days before the engines coincided again; I also doubted my ability to impinge on Moreno's hospitality for an indefinite period. My gloomy preoccupations were dispelled by the ghostly whistle I had come to know so well. Through

the jungle came a terrifying wheezing of steam which sounded like a crying baby. The engine appeared in a ball of fire which illuminated the vegetation on either side of the track; seconds later No.7 shuddered to a halt alongside us, totally enveloped in leaking steam.

Never will I forget the photographic session which followed, and although I was physically drained by the excitement, I suggested to Moreno that, as it was almost sunrise, we might proceed to Maaslud viaduct where we could photograph the Mallet departing with a loaded train. The rake was already in place and the engine was being fuelled up. We set off in haste as my chosen location lay on the other side of the viaduct. As we walked past the log cars I noticed groups of local people tearing the bark from the trunks. Moreno explained that it was being taken for domestic fuel. 'It is of no value to the company,' he continued.

Upon reaching the viaduct, I realised how uneven the sleepers were; in fact, so wide were the gaping holes between them that one had to make carefully calculated jumps. I have little head for heights and the feeling of dizziness and nausea which resulted clearly caused Moreno some concern. Although he relieved me of all equipment, it was only by keeping a superfluous and rather exaggerated conversation going that I could take my attention away from the dilemma. The view from the other side was – as I had noticed when coming up in the railcar – magnificent. The wooden trestle viaduct was a relic of American Colonial Rule and extremely photogenic, not least with the volcano looming up in the background.

There was time to compose what promised to be a perfect picture; the early sun was crystal clear and the first clouds of the day flecked the distant volcano. The train looked magnificent as it headed onto the viaduct. Suddenly there was a grinding of brakes followed by the sound of men shouting; the big Mallet ground to a halt and a brief silence was broken by three long blasts on the whistle – the disaster signal. Without a word, Moreno ran down the hillside towards the train whilst I searched in vain for any untoward incident. Possibly a log had slipped its position on a wagon. An answering whistle came from Shay No.12 and a tell-tale smoke trail indicated that she was on her way.

Following the gaze of the brakemen – whose job it is to ride on the log cars to control the brakes as the train descends to the coast – I realised the awful truth; one of the men had slipped on a slimy trunk and fallen through the track and into the ravine beneath the viaduct. A small group of men struggling down the hillside supported this explanation. The injured man was carefully examined and then carried back to rail level, put onto the footplate of Shay No.12, which had now joined us, and hurried off

Mallet No.7 crosses the Maaslud viaduct only seconds before the disaster signal sounded

to the field hospital in Minapasuk. The log train continued on its journey.

With the incident heavy on my mind, I returned to Base Camp. The injured brakeman urgently needed attention which was only available in Fabrica, and Moreno summoned a track trolley for the purpose. I availed myself of this opportunity to return to Fabrica and we set off with the unconscious man lying in an improvised hammock slung across the trolley's roof.

Despite the track, we made hasty progress for the first eight miles until we caught up with the log train. The Mallet had derailed and brought four log cars off with her, and we suffered an agonising delay of several hours before the train could be rerailed and put into a siding to allow us to pass. Although this accident marred a perfect adventure, it was but one incident in the daily running of ILCo. – a part of the cost of being a living legend. Fortunately the man survived.

Although my time on Negros had now expired, I had learnt that ILCo's engines represented merely the tip of an iceberg, for the island is known as the Sugar Bowl of the Philippines and many of the factories used steam locomotives to haul cane from the plantations. These engines were also of classic American appearance, and I became captivated by the romance of so many vintage locomotives of unusual design working on this exotic tropical island. Clearly Negros was a Galapagos of locomotives. Long before I reached England I knew that I had to return for the island had cast a spell: its beautiful people, its tropical landscape and beaches, but above all its great little railways.

My global expeditions continued apace, but few places I visited over the succeeding years held the allure of Negros, and I maintained a close contact with events on the island. It came as no shock when ILCo. closed; it could not have continued as it was. Far more disturbing was news that a government commission had taken control of the pricing and marketing of sugar. This meant lower returns for the producers, who had responded by planting less cane, thus causing a general decline in the industry. Fortunately most of the railways were still running, but I realised my second visit had to be made before it was too late.

The opportunity came when, by amazing good fortune, a BBC producer, having read my articles about ILCo., approached me with a view to making a film called *The Dragons of Sugar Island* for a new series called *Great Little Railways*. There was obviously a wonderful film to be made, and in 1981 I returned to Negros in order to work on the film's script. Having arrived, a part of me came alive again; I was back amongst people, and trains, which meant so much to me.

Ten sugar mills on Negros operate steam locomotives, and although most are of American origin, the largest factory, Victorias, uses some 22-ton 0-8-0 Side Tanks built by Henschel of Germany in 1924. The gauge at Victorias is only two feet and the railway network totals some 200 miles of track. Victorias, in common with several other mills, had intended to dispense with steam but increases in the cost of oil and new diesels has kept the old fires burning.

However, it was the American engines which truly captured my imagination, and in this respect two railway systems seemed to stand out. The first was the Hawaiian-Philippine Company, located halfway between Fabrica and Bacolod, and the other Ma Ao Central which lies some twenty miles south of Bacolod. Apparently the two systems contrasted markedly; the former was a highly efficient operation which was immaculately maintained, whereas the latter appeared to be rather like ILCo. had been in that it existed in a 'devil-may-care' state of dilapidation.

Although most of the sugar lines are in north Negros, they are not physically interconnected; indeed gauges vary from two feet at Victorias to three feet at Hawaiian-Philippine and three feet six inches at Sagay Central. The motive-power rosters range from two to ten locomotives with a total of some sixty-five for the entire island. Although the individual rosters are small, the engines remain in service through three shifts six days a week during the intensity of the crushing campaign, which extends from October to April.

The off-season lasts five months and provides abundant time both for locomotive overhauls and the fabrication of new parts – a situation which has helped to prolong the life of many engines. In common with most emergent nations with severely limited resources, the Filipinos adopt a policy of 'make-do and mend' which is applied with remarkable ingenuity. The identity of any individual locomotive is somewhat transient as parts are freely swapped around. Many engines have been extensively hybrid-ised, and their builder's plates are not likely to be correct – some engines even carry two entirely different plates! Other locomotives might be likened to Grandfather's Axe, which over the years has received several new handles and blades.

The steam locomotive's inherent simplicity and longevity is comple-mented by its ability to burn any type of fuel ranging from coffee beans to llama dung. The Negros engines consume bagasse, the natural waste pro-duct of the milling process. After the cane has been crushed and the juices extracted, the resultant fibres are dried and baled as locomotive fuel. The only flaw in this marvellous energy-saving process is that the instant the straw-like substance is put into the firebox, the natural draught created on a working engine draws whole lumps of burning fuel through the boiler and ejects them, still flaming, into the atmosphere. For this reason, two firemen have to be employed to maintain steam pressure. Nevertheless, most of the island's railway networks are run on fuel which, in essence, costs nothing. Bagasse is also used to fire the boilers in the mills, most of which remain steam driven.

During the early part of the milling season, whilst stocks of bagasse are being built up, some engines burn cheap furnace oil and, accordingly, are fitted with stovepipe chimneys. After the first month's operation bagasse is substituted and the characteristic balloon-stack chimneys – specifically designed to suppress the emission of sparks – are substituted.

Of all the lines on Negros, the one which best proves the viability of steam traction is Hawaiian-Philippine. The company is one of the largest on the island and the factory is set in what is known as the compound. This is a small town in its own right incorporating workers' houses, shops, a bank, a hospital and many recreational amenities. These facilities provide self-contained living for the employees and their families.

I had heard that all Hawaiian-Philippine engines were green, but upon arriving at the factory was delighted to see them in red livery. They had been specially repainted for the new season as their former colour made them difficult to detect when working amid the green cane. The locomotives are under the control of the transport manager, Regino Acosta, who is a firm believer in steam traction and maintains all the pride traditionally associated with a steam railway. The engines are assigned to regular crews and, as Regino proudly told me, 'the men love their engines more than their wives'! Indeed the crews' names were painted on the steeds, whilst the oil cans, tool boxes and fresh-water containers were all decoratively embossed with the engine's number.

Hawaiian-Philippine have a roster of nine locomotives, the principal field engines being 0–6–0s from the great locomotive builder Baldwins of Philadelphia during the 1920s. These are assisted by a couple of classic American 0–6–2 Saddle Tanks, also from Baldwins. The tank engines were transferred from the company's plantations in Hawaii and their job is to receive cane from the mainliners, shunt the factory area and push the cane up to the crushers.

The company's engines have the appearance of big painted toys on a tourist line, but far from being a fun railway, their work constitutes a hard, dollar-earning business and is vintage railroading played for real. The engines are officially referred to as Dragons, and radio receivers in their cabs enable contact to be maintained with the control office in the factory yard. This system enables the train's movements to be co-ordinated throughout the plantation, either in accordance with the availability of loaded cane, or with the demand for empty wagons. As Regino eloquently said, 'What conceivable use do I have for more diesels? My Dragons may be sixty years old but they are cheap to run, never break down and will easily pull 350-ton trainloads of cane.' Operations at this factory underline the wastefulness of mass dieselisation and emphasise once again the fact that steam traction still has a viable part to play in world railways today.

A three-shift system is in operation and at the end of each shift all Dragons return to the depot which then becomes a hive of activity with watering, oiling up, minor repairs, bagassing and other sundry duties. In the transport manager's office the schedule for each shift is finalised, after collation of information from all over the system. When all operations are completed, the Dragons assemble at the head of their trains and one by one disappear into the far corners of the 100-mile railway network; another shift is under way.

Regino offered me a journey on an early morning run with Dragon No.6. We were booked along the Magasa line and set off in brilliant sunshine,

A brace of Hawaiian-Philippine Dragons stand in the factory yard like fairground engines on display. On the left is No. 8, a Baldwin 0–6–2 Saddle Tank, and on the right Dragon No. 4, a Baldwin 0–6–0

hauling an enormous rake of empty cane cars. Having left the factory, we headed out into the fields and were soon surrounded by cane which stretched as far as the eye could see, every available piece of land having been utilised. It was easy to see how Negros provided two-thirds of the Philippine's total sugar crop. Dragon No.6 had a lovely clear exhaust beat and ran with absolute precision. Every few miles we passed loading areas where we dropped part of our train. At some points our wagons were urgently needed and gangs of labourers stood alongside enormous piles of cane waiting to begin loading.

The vast majority of the island's population live in villages, and labouring in the sugar plantations provides the principal source of employment. For these people life is hard; the moisture-laden cane is as heavy as mahogany and, despite the heat, the workers wear layers of protective clothing against the razor-sharp leaves. Each group of labourers have to load ten tons of cane a day in exchange for a meagre wage of 90p each – if they're lucky! This only applies during the milling season, for when the harvest is over,

A carabao makes a timely arrival at the railhead

leaner times beckon. Inevitably the villagers regard the better working conditions of the factory employees with a quiet envy.

The villagers are employed by the landowners and the cut cane is brought from the plantations to the railheads in carts hauled by water buffalo, or carabaos as they are locally known. In common with the locomotives, the carabao also runs on sugar waste as the green leaves provide his principal source of food. He is the Philippines' national animal; he is industrious and docile and will work uncomplainingly for hours on end providing he is allowed periodically to submerge himself in water in order to cool off.

If life for the villagers is harsh, the plight of the Sakadas is infinitely worse. The Sakadas are the migrant workers who come with their families from neighbouring islands to cut the cane during the harvest season. These itinerants are open to exploitation by the contractors who hire them out to the landowners. The Sakadas live in open-plan compounds devoid of basic privacy and with possibly only a solitary water tap for the entire community. Dragon No. 6 stopped outside one of these blockhouses in which two hundred people lived in squalor on a diet of rice and dried fish. Most of the men were out in the fields, leaving their wives and children to remain listlessly around the compound. I was made welcome and even offered a glass of local spirit. One of the Sakadas sat strumming a battered guitar, whilst another sat upon the balcony railings to sing a song about their homeland on the island of Cebu. The music, though stark and bitter, had a lyrical beauty which haunted me for many days. As the musicians played, the occupants of the blockhouse gathered round to form a sea of tragic yet beautiful faces, their sombre expressions resembling those found on the faces on a Brueghel painting. The elderly looked totally resigned to the timelessness of their plight; several young women suckled their babies, whilst a peg-legged man moved across the yard with incredible rapidity to join the circle.

My preoccupation with the Sakadas' plight was interrupted by Dragon No. 6 whistling up to leave. I rejoined the engine and minutes later we headed away through the billowing green cane. My feeling of isolation was relieved by a radio message ordering us to side-track to allow a loaded train bound for the factory to cross us. We headed into the next passing loop and having reset the points, our driver put a green flag alongside to indicate that the main line was clear. This enforced stop provided an ideal opportunity to have lunch, for now the sun was high and the heat oppressive. The train crew sat on the grass beside the engine and a marvellous meal of fresh shrimps and rice was spread out on the grass – a repast completed with fruits and locally-grown coffee.

The mainliner's approach was heralded by a throaty exhaust, the ringing of a copper bell and a glorious wail of chime whistling – a shimmering sound reminiscent of Casey Jones's famous Whippoorwill Whistle. The engine was working hard, yet a gentle sigh of steam could be heard issuing from her safety valves. Seconds later Dragon No. 4 rounded a nearby curve and, issuing rolls of rich brown smoke, swept past, her full train oscillating violently over the track. For ten minutes afterwards her bell and whistle remained audible, animating the silent plantation with golden tones. We proceeded to drop off the remainder of our empties and begin our homeward journey collecting loaded wagons from intermittent sidings. It was late afternoon before we reached the factory, and we ran into the yard in fine style with a rake of thirty-two loaded wagons.

After several wonderful days at Hawaiian-Philippine, I proceeded to Ma Ao Central, where according to legend, an exotic array of hybridised American steam engines eked out their days with a song and a prayer. From the time I first saw the chimneys in the distance, Ma Ao exerted a fascination, and the welcome I received from the manager and his wife, Guillermo and Dorothy Araneta, only heightened my anticipation of high adventure.

My visit to Ma Ao coincided with a servicing period, and the motley array of dead engines in the shed looked like the contents of a scrapyard. None had seen paint in years, and those parts of their anatomy not rusted over were covered by a multitude of faded, cracked and peeling hues. Yet so doggedly persistent is the steam locomotive that even these engines – battered, bent and held together with pieces of wire – were obviously capable of fulfilling their role. The mainstay of Ma Ao's fleet was four rusty American Locomotive Company Mogul 2–6–0s running with yellow tenders taken from withdrawn Baldwin 0–6–2s.

Life at Ma Ao was made doubly pleasant by my being invited to stay with Guillermo and Dorothy; they were kind, gentle people who befriended me and were delighted with our intention to make a film about their old railway. Guillermo is one of the leading personalities of the Philippine sugar industry and was deeply troubled by the decline in production. He apologised for the state of his railway, but I reassured him, saying that 'it was not only wonderful but unique; don't change a nut or bolt of it and please, never paint those engines'.

One night over dinner, Guillermo told me that Ma Ao's sugar was exported from the coastal wharf at Pulupandan, and it was arranged that I should travel with one of the trains to see this. The following afternoon I joined the crew of locomotive No.1 hauling five thirty-ton vans containing raw sugar. Our ten-mile journey was downhill and upon arriving at the wharf, No.1 ran round the train and propelled the wagons over disposal ducts set between the track. The wagon bottoms were then capsized and the sugar dropped onto a conveyor belt which took it to the warehouse.

The building was a vast structure, rather like an aircraft hangar, and inside were 50,000 tons of sugar, mountain upon mountain of it glowing a dull brown under the soft warehouse lights; it was an unforgettable spectacle. From this warehouse the sugar continued its journey by conveyor into overhead hoppers at the quayside, before falling by gravity into the holds of the ships, some of which take cargoes of 10,000 tons. At the time of my visit, the Philippines were exporting sugar to China and America, the last-named market having been greatly expanded as a result of the latter's poor relations with Cuba.

Apart from delightful interludes at the Aranetas' residence, most of my time at Ma Ao was spent on line, and my next journey began at 1.30 a.m. the following morning, when I was awakened by one of the Aranetas' servants in order to join the 2.30 departure on the Cutcut Line. It was to be an exciting trip as this line led to the base of an active volcano. Our engine was the blissfully decrepit No.5, obtained secondhand from Bacolod-Murcia Milling, whose railway operations had ceased. Having walked through the pulsating roar of the steam-driven mill, I saw my engine being loaded with bagasse; already the tender was full, but an auxiliary wagon had been added on account of our long journey. One driver and three firemen on the footplate of a three-foot-gauge engine leaves little extra space for a visitor, and so I installed myself upon the back of the tender. This elevated position commanded a perfect view and as there were no bridges or tunnels on the route, I could sit in safety.

Our procedure this time was to propel the empty wagons, the first of which was about one quarter of a mile ahead of the engine. A green light, held by a brakeman riding on the leading wagon, indicated all systems go for No.5, which tackled its load with a pugnacity not unlike that of an angry bull. The night was crystal clear and the stars twinkled with such clarity that the distant volcano became silhouetted against a sky washed in cobalt blue. Huge palm trees stood like sentinels motionless by the tracksides. Sitting on No.5, listening to the engine's syncopated exhaust beats, and watching the beautiful pall of fire rising fifty feet into the air, was sheer bliss. I felt happy and deeply at peace with the world.

After about half an hour we stopped and I was called down. 'Coffee,' the driver said. I followed the men through a thicket and into a clearing containing a wooden hut. Obviously this was a gathering place for the field workers, and a woman and girl were busily dispensing delicious hot coffee. I sat with the crew and as we enjoyed our coffee, locally-made cigars were passed around. Again a feeling of contentment descended – I was in perfect company.

Continuing our journey, I watched the sky for the first flush of dawn but my attention was diverted by a red light on the leading wagon; the brakeman was signalling frantically. Before the driver could shut off steam I saw the red light veer off crazily at right angles and disappear. There was a distant wrench of metal and we stopped amid a roar of steam. 'Wagons off the road', I heard the driver shout. The crew took several rerailing clamps from the tender, and minutes later it was reported that ten wagons had left the track and run deep into the surrounding cane; fortunately the brakeman was unhurt. I was aghast at the chaos, for if such an accident had occurred in a developed country, it would have taken hours to rectify. Filipino ingenuity, however, had learned to deal with such mishaps, for the tracks were cheaply laid without proper ballast and the heavy rains constantly undermined the foundations. Inevitably derailments were commonplace. The rerailing clamps were brought into play and some heavy buffeting from No.5 – through an ingenious system of lamp signals to the driver – soon had the offending vehicles back on the line and, within thirty minutes, we were bowling along again as if nothing had happened.

Dawn finally broke as we approached the volcano although my attention

The last of the day's sunshine as a typhoon ominously approaches over the Ma Ao plantations. The engine's cab and tender are well sheeted up with corrugated iron in anticipation of the deluge

was distracted by a distant light curving its way around the base of the mound and heading in the opposite direction from ourselves. 'That's engine No. 3,' said one of our firemen, 'she left the factory an hour ahead of us.'

It was light when we reached the end of the line and having put the empties into the sidings, No.5 began to marshal the loaded wagons. Some sticks of succulent cane were brought to the engine, and after the hard exterior had been cut away, we bit into the soft centres which were indescribably lovely to eat. Only the sweet juices are consumed, the fibres (or bagasse) are spat out. The cane provides excellent sustenance when out in the fields for long hours, but when eaten to excess on an empty stomach, promotes a contented lethargy. In fact, the effect can be quite heady and throughout my journeys at Ma Ao I was very slightly 'high' from eating too much cane.

By mid-morning we were ready to leave; this time the engine had its chimney facing the factory and was hauling the wagons in the usual way. The Cutcut Line undulates like corrugated iron and on one heavy gradient No.5's steam pressure fell too low and we were forced to stop for what is known in railway parlance as a 'blow up'.

Alongside were a clump of coconut trees and the brakeman asked if I had ever tasted fresh coconut. When I said 'no' he looked up towards the huge clusters which swayed at least forty feet above us in the adjacent trees. 'Would you like one?' he asked. 'Of course,' I replied, 'but how can we possibly get those?' 'By shinning up the tree,' he retorted with a swarthy,

Ma Ao's No. 3 out in the cane fields

gold-flashing smile, whereupon he proceeded to climb the smooth round trunk with breathtaking alacrity. Upon reaching the top, he crawled into the bushy mound and seconds later huge coconuts were raining down onto the ground in a series of thwacks. We cut them open and drank the delicious cool milk, my excitement over this ordinary incident greatly amusing my companions.

Long before we had finished enjoying the coconuts, our engine had a full head of steam; thus, having regained my place up on the tender, we set off towards the factory – the chimneys of which could just be discerned on the far horizon. Little did I know that I was about to encounter a terrifying experience.

From my position I could look back along the train. Everything seemed to be going well until I suddenly noticed that our engine had broken away from the rake of wagons and our fifteen loaded wagons were bearing down upon us at speed. I had heard stories of such events and knew that the consequences could be disastrous, as the wagons, upon striking the engine, invariably rear up over it. Flinging myself across the tender, I screamed to the driver; No.5 was blowing off and he didn't hear. I shouted again in a voice not recognisable as my own; I don't think he actually heard me, but some sixth sense seemed to tell him what was wrong, for without turning round, he accelerated the engine with all the drama of a scene from *The Great Locomotive Chase*. The breakaway wagons were only feet away and still hurtling towards us, but our rapid acceleration prevented a serious

Hawaiian-Philippine's Dragon No. 6 far out in the cane fields

collision and we felt only a gentle bump of couplings after which No. 5 drew the train to a standstill.

We discovered that a steel coupling pin attaching the engine to the leading wagon had snapped in half as if it were a matchstick. This had obviously occurred when we had been hauling under stress; however, the undulating track had enabled the engine temporarily to pull away on a short up-grade without anyone realising what had happened. But when the grade turned downwards again the runaway wagons gained a terrific momentum, the engine meanwhile having slowed down on account of a particularly rough stretch of track. We replaced the pin from a reserve supply, laughing as we did so, but no one was under any illusions about the narrowness of our escape.

I remained at Ma Ao over several more exciting days, and would have stayed longer had not time forced me to move on. It was with a heavy heart that I left the Aranetas and their unique railway system, which with the industry's general decline was clearly under threat of closure.

My journey from Ma Ao was a nostalgic one for this time I returned to Fabrica to visit Lopez Sugar Central who were working three-cylinder C type Shay No.10, built by Lima in 1924. This veteran was the last regular working Shay on Negros and one of the last in the world. The engine is said to have a chequered history having originally been built to the standard gauge (four feet eight and a half inches) for Adams Banks Lumber Co. of Moreton, Missouri. In 1937, she was converted to a gauge of three feet six inches and sold to ILCo., and eventually passed to Lopez Sugar Central sometime after World War II.

Shay No.10 is the only working steam locomotive at Lopez and is employed bringing heavy trainloads of cane down the steep mile-long gradient to the factory. She survives on this duty on account of her having superior braking power to the diesels.

Following ILCo's closure, some engines, including Nos.7 and 12, were sold to Sagay Sugar Central which was located twenty miles to the east of Lopez. I knew these engines were not in use, but wishing to renew my acquaintance with them, I borrowed a decrepit jeep in which to make the journey. The jeep broke down three times and in the event, the journey took all day. However, my perseverance was rewarded as, upon approaching Sagay, I saw the most remarkable graveyard containing three of ILCo's old Shays and the big Mallet.

As my vehicle swung into the factory yard, I saw a familiar figure sitting on a wall in front of the main office. My jeep drew up and jumping out I called 'Conrado'. He looked for a full thirty seconds in open-mouthed incredulity, 'Colins Garratts,' he said. 'Yes, I told you I would return,' I replied. We shook hands warmly and I congratulated my friend upon securing a job at Sagay following ILCo's closure.

Together we explored the graveyard; Nos.7 and 12 stood, by amazing coincidence, side by side and I mused upon how, seven years earlier, I had caught them bathed in fire. Their ability to mesmerise was undiminished, for now the vigour of their fiery stacks was replaced by rampant vegetation which sprouted from every crevice in their ironwork. This vegetation underlined not just the remarkable fertility of Negros but also the inherent animation of two ghosts which refused to die.

Not even the Philippine make-do and mend can save every engine and when all the options run out the graveyards fill up. For despite all its inbuilt simplicity and longevity, the steam locomotive can't go on for ever. Yet on Negros it must. 'We have skilled men here who could repair them,' Conrado said in defiance of the ramshackled hulks, 'and as long as the price of oil continues to rise, our only alternative is with steam.'

Dragon No.6, which seems partially dissolved in a heat haze, heads through a field of burning stubble on the Hawaiian-Philippine network

Poignant though my encounter with ILCo's ghosts was, my last memory of the island's engines occurred several evenings later at Hawaiian-Philippine. I had spent the day with a group of Sakadas at one of the main loading sidings, when I saw Dragon No.6 heading through a field of burning stubble, the locomotive's acrid form partially dissolved in heat haze. The drama was heightened by a raging sunset welling up across the sky. The burning stubble and the sunset seemed to symbolise the end of a chapter; the end of another cycle as the fields were prepared for replanting.

Watching Dragon No.6 drifting ethereally through the smoky haze with Whippoorwill Whistle blowing, I hoped desperately that a way might be found to alleviate the chronic state of the sugar industry – if only because it provides the island's economic backbone. With the factory owners getting increasingly lower returns from the government, the island's equilibrium is in danger of being seriously undermined, and the industry, like the old steam engines, remains inevitably in decline. Whatever the future holds, when the Dragons finally become extinct, sugar island will never be the same again.

GREECE
Slow Train to Olympia
MICHAEL WOOD

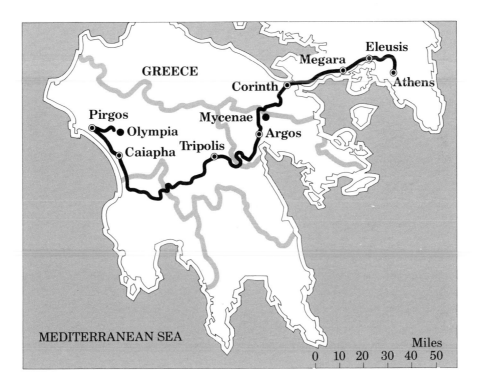

Like many northerners, I was in love with the Mediterranean long before I saw it. And with Greece in particular. Greece, it has been well said, is an affair of the heart. Of it W. B. Yeats wrote, 'Greece, could we but approach it with eyes as young as its own, might renew our youth.' For me the affair began as a mysterious longing created by those strange and powerful myths, wonder-bearing and dreamlike, yet voluptuously concrete, that are so naturally comprehended by the child's mind. When I was a little older, seductive images of an ideal landscape, seen in books, or glimpsed in the black-and-white films of Compton Mackenzie, brightened our schooldays. Then came the travel books of Henry Miller and Lawrence Durrell, in which time past and time present seemed to mingle in an intoxicating, but earthy, mysticism. So the love affair was well advanced before ever I set foot in Greece.

The era of package travel had not quite begun when at eighteen I hitched through Europe, roughing it, like so many of my generation, with no money and pots of goodwill. On that trip the ideal landscape was to be fixed forever in my mind, in a heady mixture of twentieth-century reality and the images derived from my childhood. I took the train from Athens to Olympia for the first time then – the little blue and yellow automatrice that goes through the central Peloponnese (*not* round the north coast via Patras: it is not nearly so good!) – slept in a field near Mycenae, in a copse on the magic mountain of Mistra, and on a beach near sandy Pylos, and came back to a rainy autumn in England drunk on the romance of Greece. It's not really so long ago, only seventeen years, but it seems another world. What would it be like going back today? Were the visions of youth bound to be disappointed?

Let me say at once that making the journey from Athens to Olympia again in 1982 brought history home to me in a very plain way. It is very easy to talk glibly about 'eternal Greece', about its timelessness. The travel brochures are full of it (Greece has taken over from Majorca and the Costa Brava as the number one draw for British tourists). But there certainly *is* a timeless reality in Greece, whatever the pressures are to undermine it. You see it first before you set out, in the fish restaurants in the Piraeus, in that crowded Mediterranean port crammed with the ships of all nations, from Beirut, Alexandria, Istanbul, Tyre, Sidon, Marseilles, Tangier and Cadiz – that single race, the Mediterranean sea peoples. You see it again on your journey in the mountains, in the unchanged images of Greek rural life which have been made familiar through books by novelists such as Durrell and Kazantzakis, travellers such as Patrick Leigh-Fermor, or historians such as Fernand Braudel. You *can* still meet Odysseus among the fishermen in the smoky taverns of Kythera or Crete, playing cards as he waits for the wind to change. Away from the sea too, away from the narrow coastal strips and fertile valleys of mountainous Greece, in the barren and treeless highlands of the Peloponnese or Macedonia, the poor still live their ancient peasant life; just as they do in the increasingly depopulated islands. I have seen such a life only recently in the farm towers of the deep Mani, among the transhumant shepherds of Samothrace, and among the charcoal-burners outside the decayed mastic towns of Chios. Theirs is an isolated and archaic universe. The men who return to their almost deserted native villages after years in America do not change this way of life, no matter what new-fangled innovations they bring with them from the outside world. The deep bone structure of the Mediterranean, as Braudel has called it, changes only slowly. But I think we can see it disappearing, significantly now, under the powerful pull of modern economies, as the mountain and island villages lose their populations to the big cities, especially to Athens, which now holds a third of the entire population of Greece. The old life will survive for a while yet, at least into the next century, but perhaps no longer – a way of life which has persevered from ancient times, riding the rise and fall of civilisations, ignoring 'great' events, those ephemera of history.

If you cannot speak Greek and cannot afford the time to live with the people, but want to understand the rugged contours and stark reality of Greek rural life, you need to approach the country with the eye of the geographer, the novelist, or – and this is accessible to most of us – the traveller. The journey we are to take is not a difficult one, not even a long one. The whole trip can be done in a day. But far better to take longer over it, breaking the journey when the whim takes you and rejoining a later train. The guard will write you a covering ticket, while you hop off in a mountain village for the evening. There you will always find at least one local who speaks English after spending some years on the Brooklyn water- front (or Grimsby for that matter); there will always be food and drink from somewhere, and a bed and a welcome, providing you respect the hospi- tality and give in return. If you make the effort to learn a little Greek, then of course your experience will be so much the richer.

The tiny three-coach diesel on which we are to travel is painted in the blue and yellow livery of Greek Railways, and runs on a narrow-gauge track. It looks rather like an old tram from close up. The engine is of no technical interest in itself; steam has long since given way to the little automatrice. But for the traveller who likes to get away from the familiar Greece of the mainland beaches and the island resorts, this line is a must. The train is an essential part of the daily life of the region; the locals still depend on it passing through their villages between the main towns several times each day, though as more people buy cars, and as modern roads are blasted through the wild mountains of the Peloponnese, the railway's fu- ture may well be insecure.

ATHENS

It is in the nature of tourism that the tourist seeks illusion rather than reality. The bus ride from the airport to Syntagma Square is a depressing

One of the newest diesels built by Ganz-Mavog in Hungary in 1976

introduction to the country. There is nothing inviting about it, just an arid, treeless desolation of amusement parks, blocks of flats, forest of television aerials, all a uniform grey. The air is sticky, the famed Attic light a dull haze, the sun an indistinct glow. It makes you wonder why you wanted to come. Was this, after all, the landscape Henry Miller thought 'the most satisfactory, the most wondrous, that our earth has to offer'?

Athens itself is no relief. The 'city of light, basking under blue Attic skies' (as the holiday brochures have it) is like a dirty hothouse, sweltering under a blanket of sulphurous and oily pollution. Underneath is a consumer economy gone mad: traffic, billboards, radios, touts, pimps and hustlers. A city so unpleasant, in fact, that even the Greek government has recently announced its concern about the image the city presents to the world. The affair of the heart has become an affair of the pocket.

But to come here, even with this inauspicious start – perhaps even because of it – is to awaken all those thoughts we need so desperately in these declining years of the twentieth century, with its rootlessness and materialism. These thoughts concern the values of an ancient civilisation which elevated the beauty and intelligence and potential of mankind, while also asking us to understand humanity's darker side. For the tourist operators, and for most of us, the Parthenon in Athens is the symbol of it all. Standing up there on the steep limestone hill of the Acropolis – a fortress city since the Bronze Age – ravaged, shattered, plundered and broken, but still magical. Light, freedom, democracy. This finally is what we all crowd to Greece for, knowingly or unknowingly. We don't just come for sun and sand. Here, as the brochures remind us, we will have communion with a cleaner and better world, a younger but somehow more assured world, a less envious and avaricious world, a spiritual world. But what relation does modern Greece have to this great and seemingly omnipresent past? Is today's Athens the inevitable fate of this tiny country? What *is* the Greek present?

ELEUSIS: 'THE HAPPY ARRIVAL'

Our journey will take us from Athens, across the Corinth canal, past the ancient site of Mycenae – Agamemnon's throne of blood – into the mountains of the Peloponnese, via the cities of Tripolis and Megalopolis and many smaller villages, to the western coasts. There we will travel along the great stretches of sand dunes to the healing springs of Caiapha, and so finally inland, up the delectable valley of the river Alphaios to Olympia, the goal of so many in ancient times, whose games brought glory to Greece and gave an ideal to mankind.

The train leaves for the Peloponnese from the old station of the former Chemin de Fer du Peloponnesus: an old-fashioned French-style station, with marble floors, cast-iron pillars, twirly metalwork, and potted plants along the platform. During the first stage of the journey the little train is piled with the rucksacks of the modern pilgrims, young tourists – tall, bleached-blond Scandinavians, frumpy high-school girls from Indiana, weather-beaten latter-day hippies who have been on the European ten-dollars-a-day trail for months, even years. They are crammed into every available corner of the carriages, sitting on mounds of enormous brightly-coloured aluminium-framed packs, red, green and yellow. Overhead the roof racks are stacked with more bags, their straps and buckles jangling in the faces of the patient Greek travellers. For yes, there are Greeks on the train. Obscured by all the bags and bronzed limbs of American and European youth, they smile benignly and nibble their bread and soapy cheese. There are not so many of them at this stage, but later there will be more, for up in the mountains there are still plenty of people who don't have a car and rely on the railway. The old people, in particular, seem to use it, and the kids coming back from school to spend summer at the family village. This is not a long-distance train, of course, so we are not going to meet seasoned travellers with tales of great journeys. It is a local line, and its tales are of local life, lived at a local pace. As we get away from Athens and into the mountains, it will come into its own.

The first stage of the journey was once the most famous fourteen miles

Smoke rises from the chimneys behind Eleusis

in the world: the Sacred Way from Athens to Eleusis. Every year in the autumn thousands of pilgrims were drawn to be initiated into the Mysteries of this holiest of places, in ancient rites believed to have been instituted by the goddess Demeter herself. Here Man was made aware of himself and of his destiny; he went away enlightened, and to his grave a happier being. In the thirties you could still walk the Sacred Way through fields. But now this stretch has become a devastated industrial wilderness of factories, refineries, steelworks. Massive quarries and cement works are gouged out of the hills of Attica. Among them the odd shepherd in his shanty still scrapes a living with a few goats and a cluster of stunted olive trees, their normally silvery leaves covered with an unnatural whitish film. As we round the last hill into the Bay of Eleusis, a vision of waste lies before us: tankers, shipyards, factories, and the smoke from a thousand chimneys that has turned the sky into a yellow, gauzy blur.

'The Happy Arrival'! – Eleusis, our first stop – and of all places on our journey it is the strangest name to see on a mere station sign. 'There are a lot of truly wonderful things you can see in Greece,' said Pausanias, a second-century traveller, 'but there is a unique divinity about the Mysteries of Eleusis and the Olympic Games.' Poor Eleusis! The modern world has been relatively kind to the other holy sites, Olympia, Epidavros and the rest, leaving them in their glades of pine and blue hills. But Eleusis lies disenchanted beneath its pall of dust and smoke, jammed between the shipyards and miles of gargantuan storage terminals. It is particularly ironic, because the ancients believed this once fertile plain to be the spot where Demeter first taught men how to sow grain, in gratitude to her hosts in Eleusis during her wanderings in search of her daughter Persephone, who had been abducted by Pluto. Later, when Persephone was returned to her – but only for nine months of each year – Demeter caused three months of winter to interrupt the fruitful year. The earth was in mourning while Persephone was absent. Until before the last war, there used to be two harvests gathered here each year; if the inroads of industry continue, there will soon be no harvest at all – as if Pluto has finally reclaimed Persephone to his underworld.

The secret of the Eleusinian Mysteries was kept for two thousand years – longer than Christianity has existed. During all that time, the men and women who came to worship Demeter took an oath never to repeat what had been revealed to them, and the secret was buried with the last high priest. But as elsewhere in Greece, the local people never forgot. Each harvest time they continued to honour Demeter until as late as 1801 when her last image, a two-ton statue from the sanctuary, was stolen by one Professor Clarke of Cambridge University. The people were terrified by their loss; they prophesied the wreck of Clarke's ship, and the wreck duly occurred off Beachy Head. The statue, however, was recovered and now resides in Cambridge in the Fitzwilliam Museum.

Pollution is eating away what little remains of the glory of Eleusis. It is so bad that the town's mortality rate is fifty per cent higher than that of Athens – itself one of the most unhealthy places in the world. Over the ruins the cement factories are depositing a corrosive carapace of waste, which is literally rotting away the marble. Open fields in the twenties, tiny Eleusis (population 30,000) is now the home of two blast furnaces, two steel mills, three cement plants, two oil refineries, two shipyards, two wine factories, and scores of other industries. But despite this, I never tire of coming back. Although the site is wrecked and the landscape ruined, it seems somehow still charged with primordial energy, the centre of a force field. Ideas of suffering, torture, martyrdom are not appropriate here. As Henry

Miller pointed out, in a memorable passage from *The Colossus of Maroussi*, one must approach Eleusis devoid of Christian humbug: 'Outwardly Eleusis may seem broken, disintegrated with the crumbled past; actually Eleusis is still intact and it is we who are broken, dispersed, crumbling to dust. Eleusis lives, lives eternally in the midst of a dying world.' Typical Miller grandiloquence. I *feel* he should be right, but the harsh truth is spoken by one who has loved Eleusis no less, the excavator George Mylon as: 'Even the brilliant light of Greece is incapable of imparting life to the broken shrine of Demeter. The spring has dried up; its mission has ended, and only the ruins, piled by the hand of man, remain to testify to its past greatness.'

Another reason for going to Eleusis unfolds if you go up to the lovely museum on the site, and stand on the terrace overlooking the sea. Ignore the industrial wasteland, and look beyond to the straits and island of Salamis: before you is the site of one of the most famous encounters in the history of the world, the battle of Salamis where, in 480 BC, the Greek fleet triumphed against the odds over the might of the Persian empire. As the battle began, words were spoken that have remained the Greek rallying cry in more recent wars of liberation: 'On, on, sons of Greece, free your fatherland, free your children, your wives, the altars of your ancestral gods, and your forebears' graves; now everything is at stake.' Come out with those lines over a taverna table and no matter how atrocious your Greek, you will have friends for life! They were written by Aeschylus, the Shakespeare of the ancient world and a native of Eleusis. Aeschylus was one of the heroes of Marathon, and also fought at Salamis, so perhaps he had heard those actual words spoken. Or maybe he thought they *ought* to have been spoken, and in that he was right.

My first visit to Eleusis followed a student production of *Agamemnon* in the ancient theatre at Delphi. ('Speak me some!' cried the local postman after the first night, before falling on his knees to give an eloquent rendition of Cassandra's speech, showering his head with handfuls of imaginary dust.) After that experience, a visit to Eleusis resembled a first pilgrimage to Stratford-upon-Avon. Later I followed Aeschylus' track further afield, to Agrigento, and Gela in Sicily where he died – so it is told – in a bizarre accident when an eagle mistook his bald pate for a stone and brained him with a tortoise. His epitaph, which he is said to have composed himself, makes no reference to the fame he achieved through drama, only to the honour of having been among the Marathonoi.

Imagine then my pleasure when I stepped back off the train in 1982 to find the town square of Eleusis dignified by a new statue of the grand old man of tragedy, erected in 1975 to celebrate the 2500th anniversary of his birth, and inscribed with those never-to-be-forgotten lines addressed to the sons of Greece. The present-day people of Eleusis may live in a modern desert, but they have not forgotten their greatest son. Aeschylus' younger contemporaries said of him that he wrote the right things, and wonderful things too, without knowing what he was doing, such was his love for the grape of Dionysus. He was a true Greek: fighter, wanderer, drinker, and tale-teller. So if you're ever down in Eleusis and fancy some refreshment before you retire, dusty and heated, to Athens, why not sit for a while in a vine-shaded café outside the sanctuary and drain a glass of Dionysus' brew in memory of the Grand Possessors and their uncompromising humanity?

JOURNEY TO MYCENAE

Mysteriously restored to the light, like the ancient pilgrims, we leave Eleusis behind. No tourists get off the train with me, and the coaches of the tour operators don't stop here: after all, the place is not easily explicable in holiday-brochure terms. Now the train, its roof gleaming in the sun, clatters on, as it hugs the great sweep of the Saronic Gulf where mothballed oil-tankers roll listlessly at anchor. So far the spell of the Greek countryside has had little chance to work. But once the train crosses the high bridge over the Corinth Canal – an astonishingly steep-sided slit cut through the Isthmus (first attempted by Nero, but eventually achieved in 1893) – you enter a magical land indeed, a land which exists almost as tangibly in myth as in reality: the 'isle of Pelops'. This is one of my favourite landscapes. I can think of no more pleasant way of spending a few days than leaving the beaten track here and walking over the mountains to the sacred grove of Epidavros and the wooded coast with its hidden gems like the monastery of Taxiarkhon Agnoundas; of taking the waters by the little acropolis of Asine; of sitting with an ouzo in the old square of Navplion (surely one of the most delightful towns in all Greece). All this can easily be done from the railway line.

As we leave Corinth, the mountains of the Peloponnese begin to rise, and soon we are out of sight of the sea and plunging into the harsh, stony hills of the Argolid, a hot, dry landscape in summer, where only goats and olives can flourish comfortably. Your spirits lift after the oppressive weight of Attica. It is hot but clear; the warm air smells of the soil, of thyme and basil; the sounds of cicadas (incessant from now on) and of goat bells take over whenever the little diesel is forced to slow down as it winds its way over dried-up river beds and round rocky outcrops. We stop at little halts, some of which bring a thrill of astonishment as one recognises an ancient name:

Nemea – wasn't that where Hercules met the lion? Then the landscape begins to open out between two ranges of mountains: those on the left hand are particularly impressive. We are coming into the plain of Argos, and the traveller who knows what he is looking for will peer out of the left-hand window, straining for a first sight of the legendary citadel of Mycenae.

There it lies, on a saddle between two great triangular peaks, commanding the route to Corinth, the Isthmus and north Greece: Mycenae, 'rich in gold' as Homer said. Rich too in archetypal tales of cannibalism, murder and matricide – a place of blood. The name that has come to belong to the whole period of Greek culture of the late Bronze Age (c. 1600–1100 BC) was in legend the capital of Agamemnon, the place from which he set out to conquer Troy and where he was murdered by his wife Clytemnestra on his return. The fortifications that remain date from the thirteenth century BC; their Cyclopean walls coil about the brown hill like a stranded monster, malevolent but exhausted.

MIKINE: again the surprise and contrast of seeing the resonant ancient name on the signboard of a neat and pretty station, its tiny platform overflowing with bougainvillaea. Now at last, you feel, you are setting foot in the real Greece. The noise of the cicadas overwhelms the senses as you walk up to the village under a mile-long arcade of trees lining the road and shading you from the sun. If it is your first visit here, and you have the time, book in for the night at La Belle Hélène, the house where Heinrich Schliemann lived while he dug the site in the 1870s. There, to the world's amazement, he discovered that the old tales were not just tales; that a powerful and hitherto unknown Bronze Age dynasty had ruled here, just as Homer had told. In grave shafts within the citadel Schliemann found the fantastic wealth of these barbarian warlords, who (we now know) had lived long before Agamemnon. On the walls of the Belle Hélène there are faded pictures of Schliemann and his Greek wife, Sophie, and in the visitors' book the signatures of Goering and Himmler are among those of the many German occupiers who came to pay homage to their famous fellow-countryman.

Sitting at a table in the local café, it is an education to see the flood of tourists which engulfs Mycenae from about ten in the morning every day in the season. You can see them coming out of the heat haze, about half a mile off: huge tour company buses, one after another, roaring nearer, with their air-conditioning, their loos, their televisions and videos. Some even have their curtains drawn! No one can lean out of the sealed windows with the wind on his face, as we can on our train. Up the tree-lined avenue they come, flashing past the old man patiently drying his tobacco leaves on his

The train from Athens to Olympia
crosses the Corinth Canal

wooden frames, past the women selling knick-knacks, past the men playing cards or fidgeting with their worry beads. On up the hill they zoom, while the local Greeks hardly acknowledge their passing. They may not like it, but it brings them their livelihood, and they are used to it by now. After all, it has gone on ever since Schliemann pulled the gold funeral mask off a semipreserved face, and sent the king of Greece his famous (if inaccurate) telegram: 'I have gazed upon the face of Agamemnon.' Now they come in their hordes to contemplate the ruins: in a way, they are here to worship the past.

During the tourist hours the scene on the site is predictable but nonetheless incredible. People tumble out of the coaches, blinking in the sunlight, to wander all over the ruins, snapping pictures and talking in a babble of languages. One or two don't even get out of the bus. Some come only as far as the Lion Gate, where interpreters in ten languages tell how 'Agamemnon vas a great man und a good king, but se Gods say he must be punished'. One feels that for many Westerners, especially Americans, who are used to comfort, trips like this are to be endured, rather than enjoyed. But *done*, nevertheless. Meanwhile the Greek van plying fruit juice and ice-cream at double the prices down in the village does a roaring trade.

At six o'clock the man in the peaked hat blows his whistle and starts shooing people off the hill. The last of the buses are sealed with their sleepwalking cargo and drive off. Behind them the gates clang to, the van shuts up shop. Down in the craggy gorge behind the citadel there is the tinkling of sheep bells, as a shepherd and his dog drive his flock back home. Up above, from the mountain top, you can see Argos and the sea ten miles away down the plain. As the night descends, the wind gets up, blowing around the gorge, whipping the thorn bushes, and whistling through the palace stones, where film wrappers litter the bath in which Agamemnon died. Mycenae is returned to that solitary darkness from which Budget Flyaways only ever seem a momentary reprieve.

THE MOUNTAINS OF THE PELOPONNESE

Next morning the train is there to take us on our way. Now the little diesel is really racing along the flat fertile country between Mycenae and Argos. It averages around twenty miles per hour over the whole journey (from Athens to Mycenae took three hours, for instance), but on this stretch gets up to twice that speed. We are back among the rucksack brigade, and once again the coaches are chock-a-block. A gaunt and impoverished-looking man with several days' growth of beard clambers over the legs to sell his greasy little kebabs: 'Souvlakia, kali souvlakia!' Outside the carriage are mile on mile of orange trees and olive groves, shimmering silvery-green. Argos itself is an ugly and characterless modern town, overshadowed by great bare hills, on one of which sits a huge Byzantine fortress which can be seen several miles away.

The atmosphere on the train begins to change again at Argos, for here, and then at Lerna on the coast itself, the boys and girls with their rucksacks pour off for the beaches of the gulf of Argos, at Navplion, Tolon, Mili. They have almost all left us as we pull away from the coast and enter the mountains, the eastern massif of the Peloponnese, and from now on the travellers are predominantly Greek. Even the train itself takes on a more local air, and darts along, lizard-like, looking very much a part of the increasingly wild landscape. The Greeks are mostly making short journeys, perhaps carrying a few boxes containing tins of evaporated milk back to their café in the hinterland, bringing an old grandmother back from a funeral or a marriage, or visiting relatives for a summer break in the home village. They are inordinately attached to the old village, and will often come back to it to live out their days after spending forty years on the New York docks, or as with one man we shall meet in Chranoi, twenty years in the Melbourne hospital catering department.

The mountain route has spectacular moments even in this early stretch, as it winds through a landscape broken by deep gulleys and watercourses, still flowing in the summer. Almost too soon, at the end of a great loop in the hillside, we reach the next stop at the lovely mountain village of Parthenion. Here is the life of which I spoke at the beginning: the life lived in the Mediterranean since time immemorial, oblivious to the rise and fall of civilisations, Greek, Roman, Byzantine, Turkish. It is an ancient toil, as George Seferis puts it, 'rooted in the rhythm beaten upon the earth by feet forgotten'. Here the women do much of the work while the men talk in the cafés: in traditional Greece the sexes are separate in their roles and in their society. Here are the familiar images of the Greek country – the jumble of two-storeyed flat-roofed verandahed houses, no different from those discovered intact from the Bronze Age at Thera; the brightly painted shutters faded by the sun, festooned with roses; whitewashed plane trees in the square; the cafeneion with its rickety tables where the men sit; the yellowing portraits of the patron's ancestors on the wall over the stove; washing hanging in front of the painted cupolas of the church; the holy icon that is carried around the streets every Easter; a songbird in a cage by an open door where the black-clad old women sit talking; a patient donkey shuffling up the maze of narrow streets with its back-breaking load of fire-

A typical Greek village, a few miles from Tripolis

wood; the tiny chapel with its blue painted cross standing over the spring where the women come to draw water.

From Parthenion the line gradually descends into the plain of Tripolis, which lies flat and fertile in the centre of the Peloponnese, looking like a brilliant green inland sea ringed by mountains. Tripolis itself is another colourless and ugly modern sprawl. The train climbs on southwards, out of the plain through bleakly beautiful scenery to a bare and desolate upland, where the single track between Tripolis and Megalopolis is from time to time swept away by rain or landslide. From the top can be seen the modern town of Megalopolis, one of the big cities of the central Peloponnese. Overlooked by power stations, ugly and jerry-built, it has swollen to take in the many people who have left the villages for the towns in the last ten years. 'The city will follow you,' wrote Cavafy, the greatest modern Greek poet;

'as you have destroyed your life in this little corner, you have ruined it in the entire world.' Grim words, that were anticipated even in the second century when Pausanias (the Baedeker of the ancient world) wrote of the old town, the 'Great City' which lies in ruins a mile or two outside the modern town: 'I'm not surprised that Megalopolis – for which all Greece had the highest hopes when it was founded – should have lost all of its beauty and ancient prosperity, or that most of it should be in ruin nowadays' – even then! – 'for fate alters everything: that is how temporary and completely insecure human things are.'

Whether Fate or human responsibility is to blame (and the ancients perhaps saw no distinction between the two) you feel relieved to reboard the train and to hurry away from this dismal city of the plain.

The train now enters a lush and beautiful landscape, traversed by mountain ridges over 4000 feet high. This is the final range of mountains between us and the rich plain of the southern Peloponnese. The terrain is almost trackless, crossed by only a very few metalled roads, and is in part still heavily forested, with some oaks even remaining from the primeval forest of classical times. The more familiar image of the modern Greek landscape – that of bare scrubby mountainside – is the result of deforestation of recent centuries, especially under Turkish rule.

As the late afternoon sun slants across the hills, one blue ridge after another recedes into the horizon. Game still roams the mountain tops, and occasionally you can hear the distant blast of a shotgun as the village men go hunting. Above us a pair of eagles turn slowly in the warm air. Inside the carriage two local women screech animatedly above the noise of the wheels. One of them says she is on her way back from visiting her son in the city: 'He's living like a king, you know. It's not right!' she exclaims. 'Never mind,' says her companion. 'You only live once. He's young . . . let him be . . .' The city will follow you . . .

We make a brief stop at a village which at a glance seems to deserve its name of Paradhisia, then just before the train reaches the highest point of its climb we clatter through a cutting to see another village spread over a series of hills at the top of a magnificent gorge, from which you can see the sea in the distance, twenty miles away. This is Chranoi, and I broke my journey here again, before the train began its breathtaking descent. To get off here is to find a tranquil piece of rural Greece quite untouched by the outside world, and where apparently strangers rarely stop. Here local life revolves around the railway: the track, lined by cafés and houses, is itself the main street. When the people take their evening walk – the volta – they stroll up and down between the rails. 'Most of the people in the village use

A steam locomotive at Paradhisia station on a rainy day. Steam trains no longer run on this line

the train,' one of the villagers told me. 'Any time you want to go to Athens, to Megalopolis, to Tripolis, six, seven trains a day . . . it is all the transport we have . . .'

Chranoi has a modern, Byzantine-style church and an older chapel on the end of the promontory, and typically in mountain Greece the bearded Orthodox priest is still a pillar of the community. He sits with the village men in the square and seems to join in everything, except the perennial games of cards: 'the father draws the line at gambling,' I was informed, approvingly.

Tasos Nikolocopoulos told me about the villagers. He is untypical of them in that he has spent twenty years catering in Australia, and made enough money to come home and settle down in his village, married to a girl from the next village. So he is a man with money. Chranoi people are happy and contented, he says: 'Nothing happens here, no trouble, no one steals anything. It's just peaceful . . . After work they come to the shop, meet one another, they sit down, have something to eat, and after they start to drink and sing . . .' But is the idyll quite as simple as that? Tasos is a man of standing in the village; he has given the church a new clock. But the other villagers, when they gather the gist of the conversation, are less complacent. They reveal the underlying anxiety that gnaws at village life in today's Greece; the young are either uninterested in the village ways, or not finding work, or work that is well enough paid, they go off to the towns, or abroad, leaving behind an ageing population that will not be able to look after itself. But 'people have been leaving villages since before

Christ,' says Tasos easily and with some truth. What is the Greek if not a wanderer?

Is Tasos right to be so optimistic? One fears that the villages may at last be living on borrowed time, and that the demands of modern life (and of tourism) will somehow empty them of their life blood. An old man plays with his worry beads and says little. The young men look uneasy. Only Tasos seems entirely confident that if village life waited for him, it will wait for others, indefinitely.

THE DESCENT TO THE PLAIN

At six o'clock the next morning, as the church bell calls the faithful in the village, the first train of the day passes through Chranoi, to take us onwards. In our carriage an old woman, black-hooded and looking exactly like those who have been travelling with us on all the previous days, is still sitting rather nervously on the edge of her seat, and looking out of the window, perhaps in case she misses the sight of her son or grandchild waving to her from the station of her destination. Amazingly, passengers going to work or to the shops, who are used to this trip, manage to snooze in their corners as the train now careers on a great switchback hundreds of feet down the mountain. We trundle perilously over rickety bridges spanning yawning drops, and under vegetation so low that it rattles on the roof of the train, or dashes in the face of a passenger intrepid enough to lean out of the window. You can see now why this railway is narrow gauge. Only an extremely narrow engine could be expected to negotiate this precipitous descent.

As the line starts to flatten out, you can still make out the cut on the hillside high above, through which we came only a few minutes before. Then we are on the level, and swinging to the right, and in a flash, between Desulla and Diavolitsi, the train emerges from a cutting to a wonderful vista: the lush plain of Messene stretching out ahead of us. The track skirts the plain at about 100 feet above the level of the fields, and enables you to see across to the mountain ranges framing it to east and west. Fertile as a sea, and as flat, the plain's brilliant green is softened by the sheen of the olive groves; its flatness is broken by tall dark-green pines and cypress, and by plumes of white smoke that drift up from the farmhouses dotted around. After the barren rocks and scrub of the Argolid and the wooded mountains of Chranoi, this is a third Greece, fecund and rich, smelling of the fetid warmth of ripe crops. The fields bordering the irrigation ditches are overflowing with oranges, lemons, figs, and grasses higher than a man. Our train will continue to the deep south at Kalamata, all the way to

A steam train near Kopanaki descending towards Zevgolatio

the coast, but we are going only as far as Zevgolatio, where you can take a connection to the western seaboard.

In Zevgolatio dark-eyed gipsies and horse-dealers are camped outside the town. Their low tents flap in the wind like great ragged birds. Gaily-harnessed horses stamp and champ at the bit; children watch us sulkily; a handsome gipsy woman rides past on a donkey, as if she is seated on a mare fit for a queen. A beautiful young girl looks steadily at us, her face framed by an Eastern shawl, her fingers lightly tapping a horse's neck. 'Wherever I travel in it, Greece keeps wounding me,' said George Seferis. Even more than the Greeks, the gipsies are eternal wanderers, 'fated to keep moving' as Virgil said; they regard us proudly, and keep their counsel.

Here we board another train to go west. The new engine is a heavy and ugly diesel; we are now on a main line, the Peloponnesian equivalent, I suppose, of an Inter-City going up to the big port of Patras. From Zevgolatio, the track was laid in the 1890s through a mountain gap – the only gap in this towering chain – that has been an immemorial route for travellers between the Messene Plain and the western coast. This is where, in his youth, Nestor drove his chariots back to Pylos. Now, on our odyssey, the points are switched, and the engine, dark red with yellow stripe, its sun-burnt colours matching well with the increasingly sunsoaked landscape,

One of the last steam trains enters Zevgolatio station

continues on its way. We hit the sea at Kalo Nero – 'Good Water' – where a sprinkle of white houses stands on an immense expanse of golden sand, blue sea beyond, and there is not a tourist in sight. For the next hour and a half the line follows the coast, along mile after mile of empty beaches, on the narrow plain between the sand dunes and the bare mountains of Vassae, which in some places come almost down to the sea.

Only half an hour further on from Zevgolatio, at Caiapha, we halt again, which at first sight seems surprising, as there is apparently nothing to keep us here apart from the single track, a tiny station room, a café, and a grove of ancient pine, plane and olive trees. At the weekends, however, Caiapha turns into a favourite spot for local Greeks, who come here to bathe; it is easily reached by car along the coast road from Pirgos. If, out of curiosity, sensing there must be something more here, you cross the tarmac road that runs along the railway and wander inland, you find another minor road going off towards the mountains through a grove of pines. The road turns into a stone causeway, over what looks like a wide salt lake lying between the dunes and the mountains, and there, in the middle of the lake, looming through the trees, you suddenly see the turrets of three grand old buildings. They stand in elegant and peaceful isolation, reflected in the lake, an air of unreality hovering over them. They look like hotels

Steam train with two locomotives working flat out on the climb from Kalo Nero up the
Arkadheika valley

belonging to a nobler age, but clearly no foreigners are here to stay. Built
in the twenties, they turn out to have enormous marble-floored communal
dining rooms, and upstairs, long corridors leading to dozens of spartan
rooms, or cells, each with bare boards, wooden cupboard, sink, iron-frame
bed and mattress, and shuttered window. Throw open the shutters and you
are dazzled by the blue of the lake, in which the mountains are mirrored.
Absolute silence pervades the scene.

   Later in the afternoon, at the time of the volta, the mystery becomes
clear. Stroll along to the end of the island causeway, through the trees and
over a carpet of pine needles, and you come to two more whitewashed
buildings, looking like a barracks, or a sanatorium. There an old black-
clad woman sits on a stool in every doorway, talking to the clusters of old

men and women who walk slowly up and down. This is a place for old people, who come to take the thermal springs which flow from the mountain on the other side of the lake, and which supply the lake itself. The old people have risen in the late afternoon after their siesta, to take the air and sit and talk. A group of women chatter as they crochet a bedspread for the wedding of a young couple. A joke about the prowess of the young man who will sleep under this bedspread has them all cackling gleefully and knowingly.

Behind the hostels stands a little whitewashed Byzantine-style church, its bell-rope looping down from the belfry above the main door. Inside, out of the sun, lingers the fragrance of incense, and under the solemn faces of the icons, rows of wax models of afflicted limbs are laid out, in the hope of attracting the blessing of a cure.

Come back in the early morning – or stay overnight and awaken to the shuffle of feet along the wooden corridors – and at about six o'clock, when mist hangs over the lake at sunrise, you will witness a strange and ghostly scene. The bell of the little church is tolling as groups of old people queue up on the jetty, where a ferry is moored ready to take them away across the lake. The boat pulls silently away from the shore, past the nodding reeds and out on to the desolate water; for a moment you can almost imagine that they will never return. But this is the ancient myth in reverse, and the ferryman on this lake takes them not on their final journey, but on a kinder one, to renew their youth. In the mountains across the lake they will immerse themselves for two hours in the healing springs, before returning to breakfast, walk, siesta, talk and sleep for another day.

Caiapha is one of those places off the beaten track in Greece which leaves the traveller with haunting images. But it seems that the ancient rituals here are soon to be ended; the hostels are to be taken away from the old people, and handed over to the tourists.

OLYMPIA: JOURNEY'S END

From Caiapha to Pirgos takes half an hour or so, and here we meet up with the rucksack brigade once more. They are crowded on to the platform at Pirgos, ready to join the train for the last lap of our journey. Once more the train's clientele is divided between locals, who use it to reach the villages on the way up the Alphaios valley, and foreigners making the pilgrimage to the sanctuary at Olympia.

Lying by the side of the track outside Pirgos are some old abandoned steam engines, rusted and covered with weeds, which once chugged up and

Station platform at Pirgos with steam locomotives and railcar bound for Olympia

down this line. The '2' type 2–6–0 in various forms was the principal source of motive power for the metric-gauge network on the Peloponnesus.

The last stage of the journey is, if possible, the most beautiful of all. From the little halt at the river mouth, the train cuts up the valley of the Alphaios, through the countryside the ancient Greeks called Arcadia, the name that has come to stand for all ideal landscapes.

> Sit down in the shade of this fine spreading laurel,
> draw a welcome drink from the sweet flowing stream,
> and rest your breathless limbs from the harvesting
> here, where the West wind blows over you[1]

wrote the Arcadian poet, Anyte. And the Alphaios valley is a truly wonderful place: a very wide (a mile at this point), meandering river valley between ranges of hills covered with pine and especially cypress. The cypress groves give the landscape its distinctive and irresistible appeal, lush and green even now, as the river flows strongly even at the height of

[1]Trans. Sally Purcell

82

Railcars at Olympia Station

summer. At each little station the train deposits its quota of local people –
such as the housewife returning from Pirgos with a new outfit bought at
the one department store in the town – until we arrive at the station of
Olympia itself. Here the rucksack brigade pours off for the last time.

This is the end of our journey, and also the end of the line. The railway
was never pushed further up the Alphaios valley, though surely it would
not have been a difficult task to drive it the short way through to Tripolis.
But it is a good thing it was not. At least in this way the valley above
Olympia is left in its Arcadian tranquillity. The train comes to a halt in a
lovely old station, which looks rather like a museum, with its classical
portico. The red-capped station-master sees everyone off and then goes
into his office to fill in his time sheet. If you walk to the very end of the
track, past the last overgrown rails and the buffers, and look over the
fence, the valley of the Olympian sanctuary spreads before you; the sound
of cicadas chirping and the smell of pine resin floating up on the warm
wind are overwhelming.

Round the corner, your reverie is rudely interrupted, as you are returned with a jolt to the summer madness you hoped you had left behind in

The rediscovered sanctuary beneath the trees at Olympia

Athens. Restaurants, a self-service café, hordes of knick-knack shops, chic jewellery boutiques, even a disco, serve the tourists who pour in in their coaches to spend a day and a night here. But unlike Athens the modern village of Olympia is redeemed by the shade of the trees which line its streets. Sitting under them, the big sell is somehow made bearable, and the place itself is not so large that it has taken over the whole landscape. Besides, didn't Pausanias complain that even in his day the Games' sanctuary was overrun with souvenir sellers, tinkers, stalls selling food, chicken and kebabs? Greasy spoons and sideshows? The Greeks may have invented the Olympic ideal, but they weren't holier than thou about it.

Olympia was the chief sanctuary of the king of the gods, Zeus. Every four years for more than a thousand years, from the eighth century BC to the fourth century AD, a festival including the games was held between the harvest and the vintage, until it was banned by the Christian Emperor, Theodosius. Greeks came to Olympia from all sides, to watch the processions, the sacrifices, the chariot races, the boys' races, and the 'open' athletic contests from the steep hill of Kronos on the north side of the sanctuary. Within Greece, even wars were subject to a ceasefire during the period of the games!

To reach the sanctuary, you walk north out of the town, along the main street, and after half a mile turn off the road down towards the river. There, under a wooded hill, you enter the enclosure. At first sight there is little distinguishable from the brown sandy soil under the trees. But then you realise the whole sanctuary is one vast ruin lying at your feet. Everywhere you look there are fallen buildings. The site was levelled by an earthquake in the sixth century; then, abandoned, it was silted over by a change in the course of the river Alphaios. So although the memory of the Games lived on in the work of poets and historians, the actual site was lost for centuries until, in 1720, it was rediscovered first by the Bishop of Corfu, and then more conclusively by an Englishman, Richard Chandler. In the 1880s the Germans began the excavations which have gone on through this century, and which have yielded some of the greatest artistic treasures of the ancient world. To see the friezes and pediment sculptures from the Temple of Zeus is to confront one of the greatest civilisations of the world at its coming of age, robust, virile and self-confident, the *Oresteia* of Aeschylus in stone, as it has been described.

Olympia offers nothing so spectacular as the Parthenon, but the combination of ruins, landscape and vegetation has a peculiar beauty. Here if anywhere one is led to think of the transience of even the greatest works of man: the Temple of Zeus, for instance (whose cult statue by Pheidias, one of the Seven Wonders of the World, was carried off by Theodosius to Constantinople), lies completely overthrown, barely one stone standing on another. The segments of huge pillars have been knocked over like so many piles of draughts, as if by a playful giant hand. Alongside, the stadium, the state treasuries, other temples and porticoes all lie in fragments under the canopies of pine.

It is a good journey's end, the glade of Olympia. For us it is easy to idealise the spirit in which the Greeks held their Games, in which man's intellectual and moral achievement was mirrored in physical beauty and perfection: but it remains an ideal nonetheless. Does the past bear any relation to the present? Do the ancient values have any meaning for contemporary Greece, and for ourselves? 'And I too was in Arcadia': so runs the ambiguous reminder. The ancients believed that in the grace of the gods there is a kind of compulsion, and that in the end, they force their wisdom on us. And then we begin our journey all over again.

POLAND

The Other Poland

LYN WEBSTER AND
COLIN GARRATT

Nasielsk narrow-gauge station. A shack and some tracks on the flatlands of Mazovia, in a region which was so poor in the olden days that it is said the aristocrats went as hungry as the peasants. It is six o'clock in the morning and the sun is already hot enough to draw moisture out of the earth, so that the earth steam mingles with steam from the little 'chukcha' as she is prepared for the day's work. The glory of steam is not evident here. To get this engine ready is hard, filthy, back-breaking work. The men doing it look grey-faced, weary. The 'chukcha' herself is battered, brown, rusty. Everywhere underfoot there is stinking rubble. The day is going to be too hot for comfort. Poland is sweating under a heatwave. There is martial law and strict rationing of food, drink and petrol. A curfew is in force and the internment camps are still half full.

It was into this grim atmosphere that we plunged when we came to

Poland to explore her narrow-gauge network and to find out what life is really like there, behind the headlines and the newsfilm of queues and demonstrations. And, as it turned out, travelling on the little lines which penetrate deep into Poland's legendary countryside was a marvellous way of catching the country and its people unawares and seeing the unofficial side of things.

And so one morning we found ourselves sprawling on the prickly, desiccated grass at Nasielsk, waiting for the loco to back up to her carriages. Someone was desultorily playing a harmonica. Two small children were herding a flock of ducks across the line. Some elderly gentlemen, already drunk at this early hour of the morning (or were they still drunk from the night before?), staggered across the fields and onto the train. The stationmaster, Josef Zawadski, who looked like a film star in his splendid uniform, gave us some anonymous Polish sweeties in faded lilac wrappers, of which the only thing that could be said was that they were sweet. There was a feeling of being between two worlds, between town and country, between somewhere and nowhere, in a marginal, magical place where time slows right down and stops. Perhaps Nasielsk station was guarding the crack between the worlds, perhaps the 'chukcha' was coming to transport us all into a timeless realm of endless, idyllic pre-war summer. . . .

The locomotive's actual brusque arrival shattered the reverie. There was a momentary flurry of activity as people who had fallen asleep on the grass woke up suddenly and jumped into the train before we glided off into the sleepy green countryside. The line was built after the war to carry the citizens of Nasielsk to Pułtusk only thirty-six kilometres away. Why anyone would want to go to Pułtusk is a mystery, and anyway there's a road and a bus which gets there quicker, but people do travel on the train – one million of them every year at nine and a half złotys (five pence) a time. The train sways and jiggles on its wobbly track in a dead-straight line, over dead-flat fields, and takes nearly an hour and a half to reach its destination.

Not that there was anything old-fashioned about our engine for it was one of the very latest in Polish steam traction; one of the ubiquitous Px48 0–8–0s built as a standard type for Poland's 750-millimetre-gauge lines. Many of the country's narrow-gauge systems were built to 600 millimetre, but after the Second World War the Polish State Railways (PKP) adopted a policy of partially regauging to 750 millimetre and in an attempt to standardise upon the plethora of varied and ageing steam locomotives the Px48 was developed as a modernised version of the Warsaw-built Px29s of the 1920s. A total of 101 Px48s were built between 1949 and 1955 and all came from the great Polish locomotive builder Chrzanow Fablok. In addition, ten Px49s were built which were identical except for their six-wheeled tenders as opposed to the eight-wheeled ones of the Px48. The Px49s were intended for export to Yugoslavia but the shipment was not made and today some remain in line service whilst others have gravitated to sugar factories for a further lease of active life. Some Px48s have been regauged to operate on Poland's 785-gauge and metre-gauge lines and today they dominate the narrow-gauge scene throughout the country, having successfully replaced dozens of older designs – a process aided and abetted over recent years by diesel locomotives built either in Poland or Romania.

It is expected that the Px48 will see many more years of service; they are still being given major overhauls and many of the crews – though admitting that work on steam locomotives is hard – infinitely prefer them to diesels, whose vagaries in performance greatly outweigh any superficial advantages.

As our forty-ton Px48 pulled us through the countryside, we became aware of the colours – green and yellow and blue . . . field after field after field of corn, the occasional clump of trees floating past, always the vast, deep sky, men and women and children and old grannies working, steam from our 'chukcha' streaming across the landscape, making it all look faded and far away and dream-like. And of course this *is* the heart of the Polish dream – the slavonic word 'pole' means 'field', so the Poles are literally 'the people of the fields'. For centuries the Polish peasant has cultivated his land and for centuries his crops have been trampled by the boots of invading armies – Russians from the east, Germans from the west, further back in time, Turks, and before them every sort of marauding barbarian on his way to other conquests in Europe or Asia.

For most of the last century, indeed up until the end of the First World War, Poland did not exist at all, but was parcelled out between Germany, Austria and Russia. These Mazovian fields belonged to Russia, whose tsarist rule was the cruellest and most neglectful of all, albeit that the Russians of *this* century marched across these fields to 'liberate' Warsaw from the Germans during the war. The Poles have little reason to love either the Russians or the Germans, but they do seem to reserve a little extra bit of bile for the Russians. The drunken old gentlemen on the train confirmed this for us. One of them had been good friends with a German soldier during the war – Gustav, who liked a drink and would go through hell for you. 'Through hell but not behind the Russian lines!' he said, and his comrade chortled in agreement.

And it was true that, looking around the people travelling on the train, most of them were of a Germanic type – blue-eyed and fair-haired, the women bonny and buxom, and children angelic. This struck the German invaders during the war, when they made a point of removing the Aryan-looking children from their parents and sending them off to Germany to help produce the master race. The Slavs have a quite different feel about them – slanty eyes, sulky lips, and impenetrable psyches. Our interpreter, Marinka, was one, and when she was unhappy, although her mouth would smile and acquiesce, her brown eyes would darken and fill with sorrow. That day she was sulking a little because she did not like trains and was thinking only of our arrival in Pultusk. She needed some flat sandals for the summer and there were none to be had in Warsaw. It wounded her proud and elegant spirit to be wearing old-fashioned high-heeled ones.

Perhaps the Poles bear their great sorrows so equably because they concentrate mostly on ameliorating their minor ones – such as finding a way to get hold of shoes, vodka, coffee, or petrol without coupons. And they diminish their great sorrows by making them ridiculous – martial law has thrown up a particularly harsh brand of black humour. For example: a man is going home one night on the train. It is ten to ten and the curfew begins at ten. Two soldiers get on, and one pulls out his gun and shoots the man dead. 'Why did you do that?' asks the other. 'Well, the train's running five minutes late, and he'd never have made it home by ten o'clock.'

From the purgatory of present-day Poland the little train took us deep into paradise. It transported us like a time machine back into a medieval land where horses wait patiently in line for the blacksmith to shoe them, where travel which is not by train is by horse and cart, where everything is done at slow pace and by hand. The countryside is always there, always the same, no matter what happens in the towns and cities. One of Poland's most famous poets wrote:

> Let there be war the whole world over
> As long as the Polish countryside is quiet,
> As long as the Polish countryside is calm . . .

They tried to collectivise agriculture here, but it mostly failed because the small farmers just would not co-operate. We heard a story of how a keen young agriculturalist visited a rural area after the war to introduce the concept of collectivisation to the local people. But as soon as he referred to them as 'peasants' they all walked out in disgust, saying that they were none of them peasants, but of aristocratic stock, and they were not going to co-operate in a system which would mean their daughters working in the same fields as peasant lads.

We got off the train halfway along the line to explore, and stumbled across the children of a family who had fulfilled the classic Polish dream – withdrawal from the harsh realities of city life into a kind of inner exile in the countryside. Margarete and her husband had moved here from Warsaw into their two-roomed cottage four years before. There was no running water or electricity, and, like many Polish homes, theirs seemed unbearably cramped to us. In the summer when their children and grandchildren are staying there must be at least three to a bed. But there was a stream at the bottom of the garden where Margarete was washing the potatoes for dinner. There was fresh milk for the children from the cows every day (it is very difficult to get milk in the towns) and the woods were full of wild raspberries and blackberries. These people had taken a private, inner road to freedom.

From their house we watched the steam locomotives and their carriages scudding along under the vast, East European sky. Clouds looked different above this great plain – whiter, more luminous, and the countryside, although beautiful, was melancholy. At one point along the line we noticed that the cornfield had caught fire, from the cinders scattered by the train. It would be the third time that day the local fire-engine had been called out to deal with fires started in that way.

The large number of fires is hardly surprising, for the steam locomotive is an incorrigible arsonist, but in spite of this Poland remains Europe's finest haven for steam traction. There is at present a national policy to dieselise or electrify but so dense and superbly utilised is the country's railway network that it will be many years before the fires are finally extinguished. Neither is it entirely out of the question that Poland will recommence building steam. Poland's landscape is not littered with abandoned railway earthworks as is the case in most Western countries. In accordance with socialist principles, Poland's public transport is highly developed and the possession of a motor car is a luxury to which few manage to aspire.

Indeed, travelling towards Pułtusk on our 'chukcha' that morning we realised that ours was but a little train in a country of little trains, for Poland, apart from being a paradise for steam, has a far greater narrow-gauge mileage than any other European country. And what a history the railways have for the train enthusiast, for when Poland emerged as a free state in 1919 she inherited lines from the Austro-Hungarian Empire, Germany and Russia. Many of these lines had begun life as 600-millimetre German military railways. Upon the formation of the PKP in 1919 further diversity was added to the inherited types by the Polish locomotive industry from such firms as Chrzanow Fablok and Warszawska of Warsaw.

Despite the introduction of the Px48s, many old-timers remain, and in addition to the locomotives for narrow-gauge routes there are engines for industrial use in such establishments as sugar factories (Poland has twenty-five), coal mines, steelworks, stone quarries and gravel pits and forestry lines on which we were soon to have some exciting adventures. Even when such lines as Nasielsk–Pułtusk are dieselised, some of the passenger-hauling Px48s will find alternative employment in industry.

Pułtusk. The end of the line. It did not feel like a destination worthy of the train. Once the passengers were dispersed there was nobody about except an old man selling wrinkled apples and unripe tomatoes outside a grocery shop which seemed to contain little but crates of fizzy drink. It was uncannily quiet, with a quiet you only find in a British town if a big match is on the television – or a royal occasion.

The marketplace had once been grand but now its picturesque tenements, made of dirty, roseate stone, had a blind, shuttered appearance. The few people who were hanging around gave us hard, defiant looks. The Poles are a proud people who do not like having their humiliating poverty gawped at by foreigners. Marinka sulked too. There was no shoe-shop and she was depressed and embarrassed by this evidence of her country's decay.

The only sign we encountered of money being spent on Pułtusk was in the reconstruction of the town's old castle – as a holiday home for 'Polanians', that is émigré Poles returning from abroad to bring money or business to their native land. The country needs their help, their dollars, so they at least must be properly looked after.

We ate a dismal meal in Pułtusk's one café. There was a choice between 'Bigos', a kind of cabbage stew with bits of meat floating in it, or boiled chicken in aspic. The catch was that whichever one you chose, it was the wrong one! Poland's state-run restaurants are mostly of this standard, but happily we did discover that there are a few privately-run places, usually off the beaten track, where the food can be excellent, and the waitress has some stake in being nice to you. This situation is typical of the Polish dual standard. *Officially* you can get nothing, nothing is available, but *unofficially* if you have dollars or something tasty off the back of a lorry to swop, everything's available.

The black-market mentality is at its most blatant in the big cities, as we found when we stopped in Warsaw on our way down south to find our next little line. In the hotels there you can hand over dollars to a waiter and get back złotys at four times the official rate, folded in a white napkin and handed to you on a silver salver. One of its uglier manifestations is the presence of scores of girls and women in the bars of all the big hotels, day and night. They are prostitutes of course, but not necessarily professionals. One young woman we talked to was a nurse during the day, but she sold herself at night to the well-off Arabs (who, some say, come to Poland specifically for cheap sex) as this was her only way of getting some dollars, and dollars are the only means of getting anything apart from life's basics in Polish shops. The foreign currency shops, called 'Pevex', are stuffed with goods which are rationed or unobtainable elsewhere – litre bottles of malt whisky, French perfume, American cigarettes, Swiss chocolate, tights, tee-shirts and coffee. It was sad to see that, on the whole, the only people who used these shops were foreigners and shady-looking characters who'd no doubt come across their dollars in dubious ways.

While we lingered in Warsaw renewing our visas we became aware of a strange mixture of emotions fizzing in the air. The anniversary of the Warsaw Uprising was approaching, and also banned Solidarity's second birthday. There were rumours of internees being released from the camps but no hope of martial law being lifted. The heatwave continued. A heavy, angry sadness hung over the city, and even our investigation of Poland's railways could not provide us with an escape from that melancholy.

It is inevitable that railways will reflect a nation's political upheavals and turmoils in the same way that they mirror its economic development. Even the briefest study of Polish railway history emphasises the country's tragic past. The PKP came into existence following the liberation of Poland after the First World War. Before this, railways were extensively developed in each of the annexed regions having been commenced in each case during the 1840s, but naturally development was in accordance with the interests of the ruling states. One of the costs of Poland's emergence in 1919 was the almost total destruction of the railway network, and the newly-formed PKP undertook, with herculean effort, to rebuild the network on the one hand and unify it to the needs of the new Poland on the other. No sooner was this daunting task completed than the network was, once again, brutally ravaged during the Second World War.

Such traumas bequeathed a rich railway legacy and it would be tragic if Poland had not made adequate provision for a national railway museum. Interestingly, Poland established a railway museum in 1928 as part of the Museum of Communications which incorporated railways, inland water transport and roads, but this museum shared the fate of the majority of cultural institutions of this type and was plundered and burned by the German occupiers after 1939.

The finest surviving example of the Polish school of locomotive design is this handsome standard gauge Pt47 class 2–8–2

The present museum, which is housed in the building of Warsaw's Gtowna station close to the city centre, has attracted considerable attention from railway enthusiasts in many countries. Established in 1972, this museum is solely for railways and consists of two principal parts; the locomotive collection which stands in the yard outside and a large exhibition hall housing many relics, paintings and models. Very few of the locomotives have been renovated but this barely detracts from their interest value. Most are of standard gauge and the older exhibits reflect a rich legacy of Austrian and Prussian designs – some of which Poland continued to build after 1919 until a Polish school of design emerged. Polish designs, though German-orientated, have a clarity of outline which lies between the German and British aesthetics. This is well demonstrated by the PU29

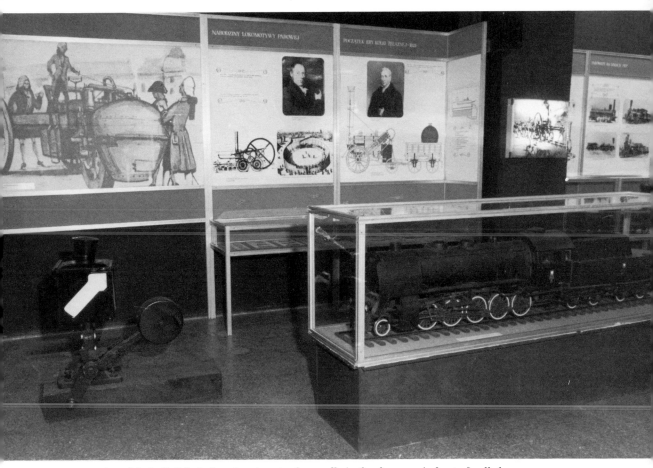

A model of a Polish-designed engine stands proudly in the showcase in front of wall plaques depicting the origin of railways in England, with particular reference to Trevithick and Stephenson

4–8–2, three of which were built by Cegielski of Poznan for express passenger work in 1930. These were, in essence, larger relations of the extremely handsome Pt47 2–8–2s which handle many fast and semi-fast trains in Poland today. The most dramatic exhibit is the Pm3 streamlined German 03.10 Pacific – one of a batch received in reparation packages after the Second World War. Other exhibits include an armoured train – unfortunately diesel – and a rare Single 2–2–2 tank of class Oka1, ostensibly Lithuanian, but possibly of Latvian origin. This remarkable survivor was almost certainly the last Single to work in the world and was active on the PKP until the 1960s.

The exhibition hall contains many superb models of Polish locomotives set in glass cases and a most striking display of colourful and ornate railway trade union flags from the 1919–39 period. The walls are decked with huge photo reproductions of all aspects of Polish railway history, although full recognition to the mother country of railways is given by a colourful back-lit transparency enlargement from a painting depicting Trevithick's first locomotive of 1804 hauling its pristine train along the Penydarran tramway in South Wales. Stephenson's *Rocket* of 1829 is also depicted in detail and heralded as the precursor of the mainstream of steam-locomotive development.

Such beautiful exhibits contrast with a photo enlargement of Nazi victims being carried to concentration camps in cattle wagons with barbed wire over their side vents. The photo reminded us of one of the few occasions in history when trains have been wrongfully used. The dazed and anguished expressions on the faces of the occupants peering through the wire were so poignant as to haunt us for days, though one cannot be anywhere in Poland without a brooding awareness of its Nazi past and the Russian liberation which led to its 'socialist' status today.

The museum's new curator, Zbigniew Tyszko, is hoping to introduce a working relationship with Poland's railway enthusiasts, who sadly play little or no part either in the Warsaw museum or in the regional ones we were to discover. Tyszko recognises that the private enthusiast is a vital custodian of his country's history and in Poland there is so much to preserve if only the necessary flair and enthusiasm can be harnessed. We dearly wanted to invite Tyszko and his colleagues, Haley and Krakowski, to England, to show them the incredible achievements made in railway preservation. Tyszko had just written to General Electric in London with a request for exhibition material relating to that company's involvement in Poland's first railway electrification scheme, in readiness for a fiftieth anniversary exhibition to be staged in the museum in 1984. But that summer passports were as hard to come by as sandals for Marinka. The government was expecting trouble and, sure enough, the first wave was breaking by the end of July.

One night – it was the eve of the anniversary of the Warsaw Uprising – we were walking across Victory Square to the grand old Hotel Europaiski for dinner. We stopped to watch the people around the cross of flowers and candles. As usual they circled the cross slowly, singing the new version of the national anthem which put Walesa's name in place of the old hero, Dombroski's. Women placed and lit new candles, young men boldly inserted pictures of Lech Walesa amongst the more conventional religious tokens. The soldiers on guard duty nearby stood well back, bored and easy. Then, as the sun began to sink behind the old city, it seemed as if a magic bell had

YUKON Steam train leaving the tiny settlement of Fraser, high up on the Pass

NEGROS Up at Maaslud in the early hours. Mallet No.7 and Shay No.12 stand side by side bathed in fire

Opposite NEGROS Shay No.10 of Lopez Sugar Central heads through banana groves

Overleaf NEGROS Against a raging sunset Hawaiian-Philippine's Dragon No.6 heads to the factory with a loaded train

GREECE Engines No. 7108 and No. 7721 climb away from Diavolitsi

GREECE Two steam engines, No. 7108 and No. 7721, catch the last of the sunset

Overleaf GREECE A MacArthur 2–8–2 lies abandoned as a railcar heads across a viaduct towards Tripolis

PORTUGAL An 0–6–0T lies in the sunshine at Regua

Previous page POLAND The Children's Special running as a 'mixed' on the section between Znin and Gasawa, past wayside banks of dog roses

PORTUGAL The 2–4–6–0T rounds a curve, pulling the Chaves to Regua train

ECUADOR Loaded steam train with passengers leaves Sibambe and heads for the Devil's Nose

ECUADOR No. 44 is inspected at Huigra station

Overleaf ECUADOR. A 'mixed' train heads through the rice fields

ECUADOR No. 53 climbs up towards the Devil's Nose

sounded which brought waves and waves of people sweeping into the square from every side of town. Soon the whole vast square was packed with a highly emotional crowd, all there to commemorate the death of their city, a death which the Russian forces, supposedly allies, did nothing to prevent. And now, of course, these young soldiers (looking more and more wary as more and more people streamed into the square) were there to enforce the martial law which these same Russians had 'made necessary' in Poland today.

Inside the Hotel Europaiski a sedate bourgeois wedding party caroused and the cynical waiters gave the well-off foreigners dining there good service hoping they would want to exchange black market dollars with them later. In between each course we went out to check on what was happening in the square. Two elements were causing the military the most trouble: young people making inflammatory speeches amongst the crowd, and elderly women weeping, keening and shrieking with a kind of abandoned rage. Cannily the soldiers let the women be and removed the young ones, fairly gently, to waiting vans. 'Gestapo! Gestapo!' the women screamed after them.

Soon the militia had efficiently cleared the square. The trams, last remnant of the city's pre-war atmosphere, wheeled the protesters home to their high-rise flats in the suburbs. Although the curfew had just been lifted the habits created by fear and suppression die hard. But in the old city there were still a few people around who had not yet learnt to shut up and stay indoors in time of trouble. A small, slightly bedraggled group of teenagers were singing and playing guitars on the steps of a monument. 'Whisky, my wife' was a typical youthful lament on the theme of loneliness and suffering, which could only be cured by leading a natural life, surrounded by love and rural bliss. While the singing went on a lad with a rag tied round his head and a wilting chrysanthemum in one hand, in hopeful imitation of sixties' flower child, passed around a tobacco tin collecting złotys and cigarettes. None of the small crowd of kids listening looked as if they had any złotys or cigarettes to give.

After the last melancholy chord was struck the singer explained to us that they had all just finished their final-year exams at school and were awaiting the results. Yes, they aspired to the natural life – that was all they wanted – but *people* called them squatters, pigs, and accused them of living a dirty and immoral life, so this was a *protest* song, protesting against all those who put them down. Behind the defiance you could sense a faint defensiveness – as if they knew that it was a bit passé and pathetic to be flower children in 1982. The young man ended solemnly: 'In spite of the fatal circumstances we can manage to live and be happy here. We don't need to escape to the West.'

But where, we wondered, would these kids end up? There are no health-food shops or collectively run vegetarian cafés in Warsaw or Krakow. One doubts whether much marijuana is smoked. If they were not going to leave, then they would have to conform – unless they decided to become political activists or dissidents. But they were not the type – too gentle and trusting for that. It was easy to believe that their idealism would gradually wilt and wither away like the boy's single, sad chrysanthemum.

Back in the hotel bar, sitting amongst the Arabs and the amateur and professional ladies of the town, we talked to Marinka. She spoke of the Warsaw Uprising with an intensity and depth of feeling that would hardly be matched by an English girl of her age (twenty-six) talking about, say, the Battle of Britain. Why? It turned out that her mother and father had actually met during the Uprising – in a basement cellar where they were gathered with five other members of the AK (the home resistance army), waiting to make an escape bid. Her father was very ill and wanted to be left behind, but her mother decided to stay with him and help him. They were two out of the three in the group who did make it through the sewers to safety, and survived to marry and bring up a family in the reconstructed post-war city. Perhaps because materially life is so hard in Poland, personal relationships seem often to develop an intensity rare in the West, where we all aspire to be cool and self-sufficient. Marinka, for example, expressed an unselfconscious devotion to her husband, Antoni, although they had been married four years, which chimed oddly with her typically East-European cynicism about everything else.

'Are you planning to have children?' we asked her one day. The big muddy eyes darkened and clouded. 'For two years we've been wanting to,' she said. 'But in this country – now – it's too frightening. Nobody knows what will happen. How could we bring a child into this?'

It was a sobering reply which reminded us of how bad things were in Poland. After a week or two in the country we had become acclimatised to the oppressive atmosphere, which might change from menacing to depressing then lighten to melancholic, but never became cheerful or joyful. The people's cynicism made them seem tough. It was only when we came down to the simple question of where the next generation was coming from that the truly miserable implications of their situation became clear.

Meanwhile Marinka had still not found any shoes. Perhaps she would do better in the south, while we were driving down to find the oldest narrow-gauge railway in Poland, the forestry railway in the Bieszczady mountains, a fat tongue of wild terrain which sticks out into Russia on one side and Czechoslovakia on the other. But it was not to be so. As we penetrated further south the towns became drabber and more impoverished. In Sanok and Krosno we even saw queues again, more or less abolished by rationing elsewhere. There were queues for shoes too, but what shoes! Not up to the standard of elegance which the metropolitan Marinka was searching for.

At our boarding house in Cisna, in the heart of the Bieszczady, the water was 'on' for one hour a day, and the toilets were never 'on' at all. When we arrived we were obliged to wash in the river at the back of the building. However, every day there were cakes and pudding made with the soft fruit which grows so profusely in the forests, and Cisna was the most cheerful place we had been to so far. It pullulated with campers and hikers who looked as if they were roughing it and enjoying it. The wastes of the Bieszczady really are trackless – you can plunge into the mountains and not meet another soul for days and nights. You can swim in the lakes – they are clean and sandy and not freezing cold like Derwentwater. In Cisna you can buy ice-cream and sok (very sweet fruit juice usually the colour of boiled beetroot) but otherwise there are no pubs, no watering stations for miles around. In the winter the recently built roads become impassable and the little railway is the only means of communication. Its tracks are so frail it cannot go faster than twenty miles an hour, and it frequently goes slower as it burrows through tunnels of leaves in the dense forests of the borderland. The train in which we travelled was the daily scheduled passenger, although strictly it is run as a 'mixed', i.e. a combination of passenger coaches and logs. This service leaves Cisna at six o'clock for Łupkow, whereupon the train reverses to Smolnik to run up the northward extension to Rzepedz. The train returns via the same route to arrive back in Cisna at four o'clock in the afternoon. A glorious journey for only thirty-two złotys (25p). Ninety per cent of the railway's 16,000 passengers a year are tourists. During the heavy winter snows, the railway becomes a lifeline carrying food and supplies to villages and outstations – especially over the wild section between Smolnik and Rzepedz.

The train was full of cheerful, wholesome young hikers eating apples and singing rumbustious songs. But outside the morning mist was slow to lift from the luscious rolling countryside and the dark-green forests so that, until the sun broke through, our journey had an ominous, chilly feel to it. And there were strangely few houses or settlements along the track although the earth looked rich and fertile. Why? Marinka explained. Before the war not only Polish highlanders had lived here but also people

An interesting exhibit in the logging museum at Cisna is this Px48 0–8–0. This is the type of engine referred to earlier as running between Nasielsk and Pułtusk

of Ukrainian origin – Hutsuls, Lemkos, Bojkos. There was a great deal of tension between the Poles and the Ukrainians, and after the war the Ukrainian partisans who had fought so fiercely against both Germans and Russians turned on their Polish allies and made a last, ferocious bid to win their independence. They lost. Their wooden houses, churches, whole villages along these tracks were burnt to the ground, and their inhabitants transported to places where they would have to forget their aspirations. That meant either Russia or the lands in the West which Poland had recently won from Germany. Some surviving houses were transplanted to a neat, outdoor museum in the town of Sanok. For years after the troubles the area was kept clear, but now people are being allowed back, to work and to settle. But flames from the past still burn through today's sensible, cheerful holiday-making atmosphere. The withered, black-eyed old men on the train, too old to work, must surely be Ukrainians who managed somehow to stay.

We were extremely lucky that the 'mixed' was steam-operated during our visit as our engine Kp4 No. 1256 was not only the railway's last active steam locomotive, but she was also to be withdrawn and sold over the following few months. Poland's economic problems, combined with those of the forestry railway, had forced the manager, Kazimierz Blaz, to agree to sell off his steam fleet for scrap. 'Those engines,' he told us, 'carried over two million cubic metres of wood during the twenty years between 1957 and 1977 and,' he added ruefully, 'the diesels are not their equal.' Then quite unprompted by us came the remarks one hears on railways all over the world. 'If we could obtain the parts for our steam locomotives we would prefer to use them; the problem is that today's manufacturing is geared to diesels. The theory supports new technology but diesels haven't the reliability of steam – any of my men will tell you that. Diesels need so many small parts which we have difficulty in obtaining. These Romanian hydraulics were built in co-operation with West Germany from which many parts must come, but frequently they are damaged by the time they reach us. And yet I have been obliged to sell my steam fleet for what little money it will fetch.'

One Px48 and a Kp4 had already been taken complete to Szczecin where their boilers will be utilised for heating asphalt. Three other Kp4 boilers had been purchased by farmers for heating greenhouses. 'Of course they only want the boilers,' Mr Blaz explained. 'The rest of the engine will be cut up here in Cisna for the price of scrap metal.' The engine which had worked our train was earmarked to go to the ZKL plant at Oleszyce, again for stationary boiler duty. 'That leaves two engines,' Mr Blaz continued, 'and they are here in our forestry railway museum as permanent memorials to the part steam played in the development of industry in the Bieszczady.'

The railway, which dates back to Austrian Empire times, was built in 1895 as a 760-millimetre-gauge line from Cisna to Łupkow twenty-five kilometres to the north-west. Its principal purpose was to convey passengers but some logs were carried. Further extensions were made in 1904 southwards from Cisna as far as Kalnica. In 1919, the line passed to the PKP and the gauge was changed to 750 millimetres. After World War II, when forestry interests were becoming increasingly important, the system was handed to the Department of Forestry Railways who, during the 1950s, implemented extensions northwards to Rzepedz and southwards to Maczarne. The logging industry consisted of beech for floors and conifers for export. New motive power came for this endeavour direct from Chrzanow who supplied two Px48 0–8–0s and six Kp4 0–8–0s. Although the Kp4s were designed for forestry work, they were predominantly for export; Russia received 500 whilst a further eighty-one went to China. Only twelve remained in Poland, where some were engaged in forestry work, and some went to sugar factories. All the Kp4s were built by Chrzanow between 1950 and 1959 and may be thought of as a Polish design although their tenders were derived from Finnish practice.

The locomotives worked superbly and in its extended form the railway totalled a running distance of seventy kilometres. The logs are conveyed to loading sidings by horse, tractor or truck and the railway delivers them either to the PKP connections at Łupkow or Rzepedz or to the wood factory at Rzepedz. The system with its small but pugnacious steam fleet conveyed some 85,000 tons of logs a year although a peak was reached in 1977, the last year of full steam operation, when 120,000 tons were carried.

The advent of diesel traction coincided with the line's partial decline – a common factor on many railways the world over. By the late 1970s, mature trees were becoming increasingly difficult to find and, when the Romanian-built diesel-hydraulics arrived, production was past its best and the railway was hoping to supplement its fortunes by carrying tourists. The idea of a railway museum in Cisna came from Zenon Cap, a regional forestry manager in Sanok. Mr Cap had visited Canada to study logging and purchase equipment and on his travels had seen many preserved sites featuring locomotives and rolling stock. He determined to introduce the idea to the Bieszczady and the museum was scheduled to be opened on the railway's eighty-fifth anniversary in 1980 but troubles in Poland caused this to be delayed until August 1981.

When one considers the steam locomotive's remarkable longevity it seemed strange to see a museum containing engines built during the 1950s. They looked in superb mechanical order and obviously had years of useful life left in them, but 'progress' had dictated that their work be taken over by expensive and complex diesels which consume valuable oil. 'And what of the railway's ability to attract tourists?' we asked Mr Blaz. 'Wouldn't they prefer a steam engine?' 'Of course,' the manager replied, 'but we must utilise all possible monies and once the decision was taken to dieselise a rapid sale was vital. I have even sold a couple of my seven-strong diesel fleet,' he continued with, I noticed, rather less emotion.

At the time of our visit, fewer tourists than normal were coming to the Bieszczady; the country's economic crisis, combined with the rationing of petrol, had severely restricted travel and holidays. And it seemed most foreign tourists were deterred from visiting Poland. But hopefully all this will change and the railway will bolster its declining fortunes with the injection of tourists it deserves for the line has all the makings of a Welsh Talyllyn or Festiniog.

It was a hot Sunday when we rode the little train. The mist had completely cleared and the sun was glaring through the windows. The young campers, up at dawn to catch the train, were making up for lost sleep slumped against their rucksacks, but we wanted to take the opportunity of attending a country mass, to find out if the Polish people were as pious as they are made out to be. We jumped off the train at a deserted station and joined a stream of local people heading for church. It turned out to be the village's saint's day, and there was to be a special mass held outdoors. In the vast church courtyard hundreds of people were standing under a broiling sun – the two-and-a-half-hour service was already halfway through. The lucky early ones had grabbed places in the shade of an enormous, ancient chestnut tree. The others endured the heat patiently. Small children in their best clothes played quietly, elderly ladies in hot-looking, black head-scarves endured the sun without a flicker of protest or weakness, and younger people, who, in the West, would reject organised religion out of hand, stood with bent heads, participating without scepticism.

There was no outward show of religious emotion. Throughout the sermon, a passionate tirade on the evils of abortion and irresponsible sex, the congregation's faces remained impassive. What did their religion mean to them? The Pope, Karol Wojtyła, wondered about that too, when he was visiting a southern village like this one. He asks, in a poem he wrote about the occasion:

> In the map of their wrinkles
> Is there the will to fight?
> Shadow moves over their faces
> An electric field vibrates.

And he adds: 'The world is full of hidden energies.' The poem catches very exactly that sense you have in Poland of the presence of vast energies with nowhere to go except underground, into a kind of internal emigration to the deep, fertile places of the imagination. So that it is quite possible for the Communist Party bureaucrat to bring his children up as pious

Catholics. What looks like resignation on the outside may be there simply to hide and protect the resistance within.

As we climbed back onto the train to plunge deeper into the mountains we heard singing in the next compartment. There was no interconnecting passage between the carriages so we climbed round the outside of the train to investigate. A crowd of bare-kneed adolescents were belting out a non-sense song about the rhythms of Africa. It was daft and innocuous enough until the last verse:

> I see the soldiers in their Russian tanks.
> What are they doing here? I don't know!
> But I know there's plenty more where they come from!

And the Bieszczady had other, invisible inhabitants at this time – the internees tucked away in their camps not far from the line (a group were rumoured to have escaped that day). The rebellious Cardinal Wyszynski had been kept under house arrest in a beautiful convent in these hills. Just like his spiritual heir Lech Walesa who was held near here too, on the other side of the mountains, spending his days fishing aimlessly and smoking and eating too much in useless comfort. (This sort of civilised imprisonment is a Polish tradition.) It is interesting that the classically Polish name 'Lech' comes from the same root as the word 'Lusatian', and some historians believe that the Lusatians were the true ancestors of the Polish people. We had stumbled across one of their ancient strongholds when we visited the narrow-gauge railway museum at Wenecja in the heart of central Poland.

Wenecja – named after Venice as a place of lakes – lies nine kilometres south of Znin on a 600-millimetre-gauge network opened in 1894 under German administration. The system originally connected Znin with Osno. The museum service is based around a small part of the system and operates over the sixteen kilometres between Znin and Gasawa. The journey incor-porates two major tourist attractions: the narrow-gauge railway museum in Wenecja and the reconstructed Lusatian Fort at Biskupin. Wenecja is one of those magical places one never forgets. It is set in the countryside of a classic Constable landscape where natural beauty exists in perfect balance with farming interests.

We arrived during the late evening just as the rooks were querulously preparing to roost in the high trees surrounding the rectory. A pair of marsh harriers beat the reeds around the adjacent lake and cuckoos called from all points of the compass. Wildlife had greatly increased over recent years following severe restrictions upon gun ownership during the

The last surviving example of the PKP's
Tx4 class 0–8–0T

political troubles. Fishing, however, was passionately pursued and anglers sat in partial silhouette, like sentinels around the lake.

The little open-air museum was closed until the following morning and we were accommodated next to the rectory immediately opposite. After a late dinner with a bottle of Polish wine we fell asleep to a symphony of nightingales singing from the woods around. It is at such times that Poland's cares seem to evaporate; the heavy atmosphere lifts and a perfect, but temporary, harmony is achieved.

The next day the atmosphere of harmony was immeasurably increased by the happy accident of Marinka finding a pair of very acceptable sandals in a dusty, unpromising little shop. Perhaps they had not been bought before because nobody in this remote spot yet knew that flat sandals were back in fashion! At any rate, from now on there was no more Slavic sulking. While Marinka had risen early to look for sandals, we had breakfasted promptly in order to spend the day with the engines. Shortly after nine o'clock, a whistle sounded over the still countryside as the first museum train of the day approached from Znin with a string of brightly coloured children's coaches. The engine was not the preserved relic one would find in England, but a grimy little workhorse. She was No. 564, the last survivor of the PKP's Tx4 class, a group of seven likely looking 0–8–0s built by Hanomag in 1923. The grubby little engine looked incongruous with the children's special but she was a genuine PKP engine for, although passenger services were withdrawn from the line in 1963, the system still carries freight – especially coal to villages – whilst many branches are used for conveying sugar beet to the factory in Znin during the season.

Rolls of rich brown smoke issued from the Tx4 as she drew to a stand in Wenecja station. Hot in pursuit of the train came two Orbis touring coaches which had obviously dropped their occupants in Znin for a journey by train and would wait until they had visited the museum before proceeding to Biskupin.

Following the party into the museum we were greeted by sprightly, seventy-seven-year-old Leon Lichocinski, a retired driver who, in full station-master's dress, now acts as museum guide. Apart from being a true railwayman, Leon is a great showman and, leading his entourage to the first engine, Tx26 No. 422, he climbed into the cab and in the manner of a preacher in a pulpit smiled down benignly upon the assembled throng and began to deliver his lecture. His fifteen-minute oration was a rich potpourri of railway lore which initiated children – in a land not unduly given to railway enthusiasm – into the joys of the subject. His sermon completed, he vigorously rang the bell on the engine's cab roof, whereupon the

Leon Lichocinski stands before a Tx26 0–8–0T at Wenecja Museum

children were free to run riot over the exhibits and pretend they were the great engineers which Leon had described. One of the many remarkable things about this man is that he was older than any of the exhibits in the museum.

The collection comprised eight locomotives along with an interesting variety of passenger and freight rolling-stock relating to the Znin Railway,

A 600-millimetre-gauge postal van

including a diminutive Postal Van complete with letter box. The eight preserved engines were of Polish and German design but were set in no particular sequence. Unhappily, they were pushed together in a line and had they been spaced out the children would have been able to appreciate them better.

One engine, however, needed little introduction for it represented a remarkable piece of locomotive evolution. The engine was Tx2 No. 355, an 0–8–0T built by Orenstein and Koppel in 1911 and the forerunner of the famous Feldbahn 0–8–0Ts used by the Germans during the First World War. The Feldbahn has gone down in history as one of the most celebrated steam types of all time. Several thousand were built by German locomotive manufacturers to follow the German armies all over Europe. After the war, the engines were surplus to military requirements and many Feldbahns gravitated to forestry and industrial railways. Amazingly the Feldbahn survived actively for another half-century but by 1980 they were generally regarded as extinct. However, a remark made during Leon's lecture hinted that a handful survived, working deep amid the primeval forests of north-eastern Poland alongside the Russian border.

Having seen the museum, we caught the next 'chukcha' to Biskupin. The train was hauled by the same Tx4 and as we left Wenecja Orbis coaches followed – the museum obviously rating high on Poland's list of official tourist attractions. Two kilometres out, we saw an agricultural branch of

Two locomotives at Wenecja Museum. On the left is a Tx2 0–8–0T, and on the right is the forerunner of the Feldbahns as described by Leon in his lecture

the line disappearing away through the undulating farmland and in the fork of the two lines we were amazed to see eight locomotives in an advanced state of decrepitude. They included examples from several 'extinct' narrow-gauge classes. The first in line was Polish-designed Px27 No. 775, one of only two examples built in 1929 for a line in Białosliwie. Even more delightful was Tyb5 No. 471, a handsome 0–6–2T with outside frames built for the Wrzesnia–Pyzdry line in 1913 by Borsig of Berlin as their works number 8741. Next to her stood a diminutive Henschel 0–6–0T of 1911. This engine has apparently spent its life working at the Klemenow sugar factory as their Su.6. We were unable to elucidate the reason for this 'second museum', but one can only trust that these rare exhibits will eventually be restored.

Five minutes later, having skirted the lake, we arrived in Biskupin station, from which a wooded lane leads to an ancient fort. This amazing reconstruction of a settlement which existed five hundred years BC was possible because, when the original sank into the earth, the high level of humus achieved remarkable preservation. Excavations began in 1933 and continued until the Second World War when the Nazis, having failed to prove that Biskupin's occupants were of German origin, covered the site with sand. Work began again in 1946 and today a fine museum of ancient exhibits from the site has been built close to the fort.

It is a simply extraordinary place, resonant with hope while reeking also of blood and defeat. The archaeologists who excavated it believe it must have been a high-water mark of the ancient civilisation because they found so much evidence of a peaceful, cultured and religious society. The fort is structured like a little city: a wooden palisade encloses streets, squares, a pillar-shaped temple, and long huts which housed both animals and people. It's thought that the inhabitants worshipped the Sun-God in his chariot, and they were adept at many crafts – spinning, weaving, wood-working, pottery. At night the whole family group crammed into a high bed in the hut, reached by a ladder, with the animals herded in underneath them for warmth and safety. And the truly wonderful thing, for this early tribe on their vast, vulnerable plain, was that the fort was on an island, yielding them some protection from the wild marauding tribes who were always on the move across the continent at this time.

If the Germans tried to destroy Biskupin they left behind equally historic relics from the industrial age and, having heard Leon's tales of the Feld-bahn, we determined to visit those distant primeval forests to see if any survived. Research conducted in Warsaw revealed that two forestry systems might operate Feldbahns: one in Hajnowka and the other in Czarna Białostoka. Both lay immediately alongside the Russian frontier. Our journey to this sparsely populated part of Poland was full of expec-tation but upon reaching Hajnowka several heaps of scrap heralded all that survived of our quarry. Apparently we were a year too late and the system had been dieselised. 'We had them here for fifty years,' the manager said as he showed us a large scrapbook containing photographs of Feld-bahns encased in armour during military action, in addition to pictures depicting the type arriving at Hajnowka during the 1920s when the forestry industry was being developed.

Our last hope was at Czarna Białostoka, a 120-kilometre-long forestry system close to Białystok on the PKP's main line from Warsaw to Lenin-grad. We were captivated by the wild beauty of the forests. During the Middle Ages these forests were used by the kings of Poland and the arch-dukes of Lithuania for hunting. Today, however, the forest is under state management and, despite the extensive logging industry, great pains have been taken to conserve the region's valuable flora and fauna.

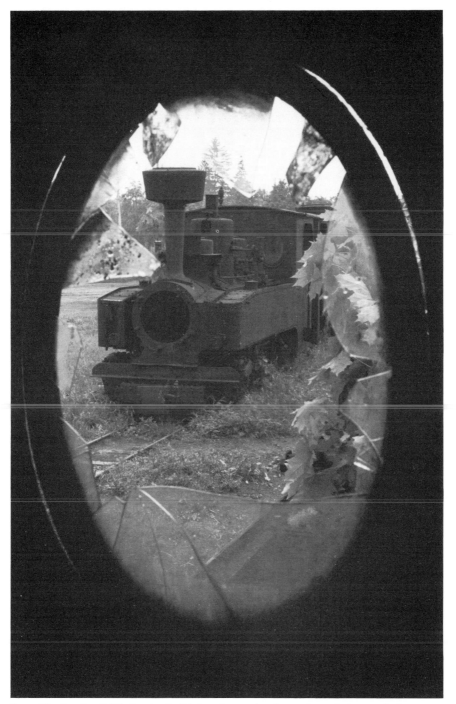

One of the derelict Feldbahns in the Białystok graveyard seen through the smashed
spectacle glass of a sister engine

Feldbahn's workplate, with date and number

When we reached the Forestry's Headquarters in Białystok, the only English-speaking occupant happened to be the Conservation Officer, Krzysztof Wolfram. We struck an immediate rapport, but before we could explain our mission, this devoted man told us tales of the 350 species of bird to be found in the nearby Piska Forest along with stories of tree frogs and garlic toads. Eventually we swung the conversation to a different kind of endangered species. 'Feldbahns,' our friend echoed, 'yes they came here after the Great War; perhaps we can still find them at Czarna – I will accompany you.' On the way we were stopped at a level crossing to allow a steam-hauled freight to pass. The engine was a Polish Class Ty42 2–10–0 – or in simpler language a German 'Kriegslokomotive' (war engine). These were the principal German locomotives of the Second World War and over 6000 were built – many to follow Hitler's armies during their conquests. It seemed eerily prophetic that our mission was for the narrow-gauge equivalent from the previous war.

Upon reaching Czarna we found the graveyard of the Feldbahn – surely the last big concentration of the type anywhere on earth for it is by definition a collective type. But all hopes were not lost, for plumes of steam issued from the yard connecting the forestry line with the PKP and there, to our sheer joy, we found Feldbahn Tx No. 1117 built by Henschel of Kassel in 1918. She was the very last survivor. All other trains on the system were being worked by East German diesels from Karl Marx City. Soon No. 1117 would be joining her sisters in the graveyard and collectively the Feldbahns would be broken up.

Overjoyed by the success of our mission, we returned with Krzysztof to Białystok, passing on the way a very different kind of monument to Poland's German past in the form of the awe-inspiring stone sculpture at Grabówka

A working Feldbahn 0–8–0T
in the primeval woodlands of Białystok

devoted to the 100,000 victims of the Nazis in the Białystok area.

Our adventure had taken us far from the little Tx2 on the Znin Railway, but possibly the museum authorities in Warsaw will arrange for one of Czarna's Feldbahns to go to Wenecja museum as more material for Leon Lichocinski's erudite lectures upon Poland's legendary railway past.

It is ironic that steam has lasted so long in Poland not because much money has been spent to preserve it but because there has been no money to spare to replace it. But it is a good irony. Sometimes when we watched the 'chukchas' scudding along the vast plains under huge, luminous skies we felt they were truly the last representatives of Poland's gallant, romantic spirit in a cold, ugly, increasingly heartless age. While they survive, albeit rusting, wheezing, barely topping twenty miles an hour on their wobbly tracks, there must still be hope for this sad, magnificent country.

PORTUGAL

Journey to the Land Beyond the Mountains

RUSSELL CHAMBERLIN

Based on an idea by Ray Gosling

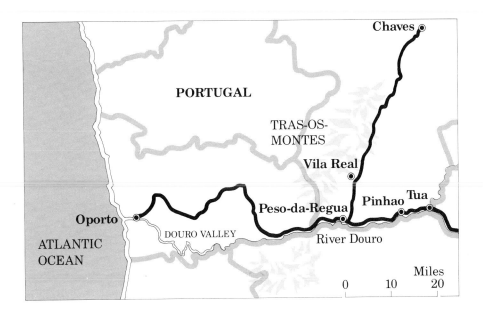

One usually hears the voice at parties. Generally it's female: frequently, for some reason, with the jagged vowels of Kensington, quacked out on a rising scale of incredulity.

'But I mean . . . You *caaan't*. I mean . . . How do you get about?'

'By foot. By bike. By bus, taxi, train, plane.'

'But I mean . . . We'd all simply *love* to ignore the car, to lead the simple life and all that. But you *caaan't*. You've *got* to be able to drive today. You *caaant* just simply ignore the car . . . and so on, and so on.

I suppose that, technologically, I must be among the last of the Neanderthals in not being able to drive a car. No physiological reasons prevent me. Or mental either, so far as I know. I just never got round to learning, and by the time maturity had set in and opinions hardened, I'd evolved a complete philosophy of hatred for the bug-like machines that turn our city streets into lethal, smelly canyons, settle like flies in every open space, cover the countryside with dreary asphalt and burn up irreplaceable fossil fuels – a million years of evolution going up in smoke.

And, by equal and opposite reaction, hatred of cars produced love and admiration of trains. Not trains as pieces of engineering so much as trains as medium of movement. Like most men (but, curiously, few women) I can delight in steam engines, inhaling the intoxicating mixture of steam and hot metal and grease; listening to the sizzlings and poppings and occasional ear-splitting shrieks; watching those endless series of purposeful movements – of this pushing that and pulling the other – which give them so remarkable an air of sentience. I can even get excited by the anonymous, enigmatic shape of a diesel engine, a kind of abstract symbol of power, its deep thunder and surging energy available at a touch of a switch.

But I know nothing about their technology. Those strings of numbers connected by a hyphen, those calculations of cylinder size and pressure and gauge that mean so much to the aficionado, are as meaningless to me as the Arabic scrawled round the interior of some superb mosque. But ignorance of Arabic doesn't prevent you enjoying the mosque, and ignorance of technology doesn't prevent you responding to this truly extraordinary invention, the most sane form of transport ever evolved and which changed, in a matter of decades, the history of the planet.

The railway laid the course of its own destruction, advancing the cause of industrialisation to the point where it would take to the road, the ancient rival of the railway which was emerging in a new and apparently indestructible form. But in its heyday it affected, directly, the lives of everybody living in the civilised countries. It wasn't, however, until I began to plan the journey covered by this account that I realised just how much trains – little trains in particular – had threaded their way through my life.

There was, first, the small local railway in Jamaica where I spent my childhood. Was it only fond memory that insisted that its smoke was aromatic, almost sweet-smelling? Not really: the engine was fired with charcoal – sometimes even wood – as it chugged its way through the exotica of a tropical island to places with solidly English names – St Anne's Bay, Falmouth, Cornwall. But there was Mount Diabolo, too, where the train would wait to meet travellers coming down by carriage over that wickedly steep ridge, and the great glowing splash of water hyacinths that marked the approach to Kingston.

The first sight of Europe was marked by the advent of a train, though a child's mind interpreted it as something of an unearthly beauty. Coming in past the Dutch coast on a black October night there was this sudden vision of an enormous, incredibly beautiful necklace of light following an invisible curve along the coast, plunging on into the night and the mysteries of Europe.

And later there was the perky little train that whisked along the rather sinister river Yare from Norwich to Yarmouth, stopping at Brundall Halt, a tiny station flower-bright in summer, its snug waiting-room cheered by a glowing coal fire in winter. I found its counterpart in Italy, chugging along a single track to Castagnaro in Lombardy, brushing its way through vineyards so slowly and so closely that one could almost reach out and help oneself to the great lustrous bunches of fruit.

And most gallant of them all, the little train that goes down once a day from Cuzco to Machu Picchu in Peru. It has to climb an almost perpendicular cliff to get out of Cusco and does so by chugging endlessly backwards and forwards, covering only a few hundred yards each time to gain a few feet in height. From only a few feet away you can peer into the windowless, dark little hovels that stud the hill, the inhabitants indifferent to the passing presence of scores of eyes, carrying on their intimate domestic chores. Not the least remarkable thing about this railway is its course for, in a little over four hours, it descends from Himalayan, through Alpine, to temperate conditions, finishing deep in a jungle gorge among banana trees.

Memories of train journeys must form part of the past of anybody born and growing up in the middle decades of the century, before car-owning became a commonplace and when the idea of air travel must have seemed as remote a concept as space travel is for most of us today. In Britain now the railway tends to be a privileged, or protected, species. Privileged – and dull – in the form of the systems that serve the great conurbations. Protected, usually by dedicated voluntary groups, in the form of small country railways run largely on the principle of switchbacks on the fairground – just for the fun of the ride. When, therefore, I heard of the existence of a small mountain railway in north Portugal that had both character and social function, and was given the opportunity to travel on it, I seized that opportunity with alacrity and delight.

First there was the need for personal orientation, to get something of the 'feel' of a remote country which I had never before visited. But 'remote'? Oporto, the point of departure for the railway, is barely one and a half hours flight from London. And have we not, notoriously, been allies of the Portuguese for hundreds and hundreds of years? And wasn't that great

Portuguese prince, Henry the Navigator, who opened up the world to Europe, himself half-English? And haven't we been drinking port for 200 years and more? And isn't there a strong English community in Oporto? How can such a place possibly be 'remote'?

Easily, for it has fallen victim to our education system as I found when I went to arrange travel insurance. The girl serving me was intelligent enough and, presumably, with sufficient education to allow her to work in an insurance office. But her first question was:

'Is Portugal in Europe?'

'Well, er, yes – on the right-hand side of Spain, going down.'

'Oh, Spain, Benidorm and that. I didn't know Portugal was in Spain.'

I left it at that. And telling the anecdote afterwards in Portugal met not with incredulity or indignation, but an amused resignation. 'All you English think we're part of Spain.' It's not quite as unreasonable as it seems, come to think of it. Why didn't those immensely powerful kings of Spain – one of whom, as the emperor Charles V, bestrode all Europe – absorb this tiny country with whom they shared a peninsula? If Ferdinand and Isabella could bring about the union of two such kingdoms as Leon and Castile, why couldn't they bring Portugal in? There are, in fact, good historical reasons – but the English have never bothered to find out about them, to gain any kind of a picture of a people who resemble them in a number of ways. Centuries of family squabbles have fixed an idea of France pretty firmly – if frequently erroneously – in our minds. The long love affair with Italy also conjures up an instant, highly coloured picture of 'Italians'. Even the Elizabethan fear and hatred of 'the Dons' has produced a firm idea which is a kind of reluctant admiration of the Spanish. Most of us know something about the Greeks and the Finns, a lot about the Germans and the Swiss. . . . But the Portuguese remain with only a vague and shadowy outline.

Dredging through the lumber of my own mind, the odds and ends of facts that any reasonably literate European collects about his fellow Europeans, I found I didn't have much more to add to the insurance clerk's pictures. The Romans had been there. Well, yes – but the Romans got everywhere. The Moors had occupied it. Well, again, yes, they would, wouldn't they, having occupied all Spain for centuries. And wasn't there someone called Pedro the Cruel and didn't he have something to do with the Black Prince? There was the great earthquake that destroyed Lisbon in the eighteenth century. And the Duke of Wellington, of course – Torre Vedras and all that. And port.

It's port that binds the two nations: port that created the vital part of the railway I planned to ride on; port that sustained one of the last, self-contained English communities on foreign soil. And as it happened I had an entry into the world of port almost on my doorstep. The train from my home in south-east England goes past some nondescript warehouses just before it enters Waterloo Station. And high above one of those office blocks, a most powerful imagery in those prosaic surroundings, is the romantic caped figure of The Don, trademark of Sandeman's, the port shippers who have been established in Oporto (where else?) for nearly two hundred years.

So to the office block I went, and in an elegant room that looked across the glinting waters of the Thames I talked with Tim Sandeman. His ancestor, George Sandeman, had been a guest of the Duke of Wellington at Torre Vedras, and during the long, long period before the troops of Napoleon gradually, grudgingly gave up Portugal, George Sandeman kept the Iron Duke's mess well supplied with the local brew. Through Tim Sandeman I learned something about the mystique of port, and about the great river Douro and the remarkable city that stands at its mouth, and the railway that winds down its length.

And so to Oporto. By air. It requires genius of a high and perverse order to turn into boredom that millennial dream of Icarus and all mankind, the ability to fly. But we have achieved it. You go up in a kind of lift and stay above a layer of cotton wool for anything from two to five hours, cramped in the same tiny seat, while you're fed at intervals like a battery hen in its stall. You then come down into a place identically resembling that which you left, breathing the same bottled air, and are then pitched out into a totally alien environment – the ultimate in culture shock. What a contrast to entering a foreign country by train – the long swan down through darkness, the land becoming mysteriously alive with the rising sun, the gradual awareness of the local language, as natives gradually displace foreigners, so that your ear attunes itself to the new rhythms of speech, the new smells becoming evident at every station, the new tastes. . . .

At five o'clock, blinking in the brilliant sunlight in central Oporto, I began the task of bringing together body and soul, sundered by movement at hundreds of miles an hour five miles above the planet's surface. It seemed a good idea to begin with the little bit of Portugal that was forever England, Sandeman's 'lodge' where the great wines slept on the other side of the river.

Oporto, like Budapest, is built on both sides of a great river, with each part somehow retaining its separate identity. This is, indeed, the fact which originally gave a name to the entire country – Portucal. For Oporto

is the Roman Portus, so important to the country that it is known simply as 'the port' – *the* port, *o* porto – while on the other side of the river is the township known today as Vila Nova de Gaia but which the Romans knew as Cale, hence Portu Cale. The *armazens*, or wine-shippers' lodges, are concentrated at Vila Nova all along the riverfront and it is a decidedly curious experience to stand on the western bank of this vibrantly continental city and see, across the great river, signs bearing such solidly English names as Croft and Cockburn, Sandeman and Taylor.

We in England have been drinking Portuguese wine for a good 600 years now – Chaucer mentions it with approval. But it wasn't until 1678 that the port-wine industry, as we know it, came into being when a Liverpool merchant began lacing Douro wine with brandy to get it home in good condition. From that evolved the complicated technique whereby a seemingly infinite number of permutations and combinations produced that liquid, at once fiery, sweet and potent, which in its turn produced that curious double image in England: on the one hand the gouty aristocrat, on the other the cheerful char – 'Mine's a port and lemon, dearie'.

Most of the British firms engaged in shipping port have, like Sandeman's, been associated with the trade from the beginning. The Methuen Treaty of 1703 virtually gave the English a monopoly of the trade for, as part of England's running battle with France, duties on Portuguese wines were substantially reduced. The Portuguese were not slow to realise the value of the liquid gold produced by those once naked hills of the Upper Douro Valley, and rigorous control limits the port-wine-producing area to a few square miles centred round the village of Pinhao – an area described, in an edict of 1932, under the proud title of 'the producing district of the Noble Wines of the Douro'.

Along the quays of Vila Nova were tied up three or four of the graceful river boats which used to bring the wine down from the upper reaches of the river. But these, alas, have been wholly displaced by the train, and are now little more than graceful advertisements, like the great shire horses still maintained in Britain by some brewers.

Nicholas Heath, Sandeman's export manager, was waiting for me. His father and grandfather had been in the port-wine business. He himself was born in Portugal and, though he went to school and university in England, has never lived there, and despite a quintessentially English manner, has no desire to live anywhere but in the country of his adoption. He is, in short, a typical member of the English colony which, dwindled now to around 500, has been established in Oporto for a good two centuries. They have their own club, the so-called Factory House or Feitoria Ingleza, a

Barrels of port wine at Cockburn's
Wine Lodge

A *rebelo* with wine barrels on the River Douro

massive granite building erected in the 1780s a stone's throw from the birthplace of that half-English prince, Henry the Navigator. Here each Wednesday, the members of the British Association of Port Wine Shippers meet at a lunch which is at once ceremonial and friendly, rather like dining in hall. Unlike their equivalent in Spain, the English colony in Oporto has preserved its cultural identity. Altogether, it's rather ironical that it is in Portugal, the land of our oldest ally, that something of the values of the British Raj should still be kept alive.

We stood talking in a room overlooking the Douro as the sun set, touching the fantastic city on the other side of the river with deepest gold, setting the stepped towers and terraces, the vast and delicate bridge, the massive cathedral that acts as a crown – setting them all against the deepest velvet. The room we were in was a surrealist mixture of bottle party and austere laboratory. There were dozens upon dozens of bottles of various stages of fullness, standing upon shelves and benches, each containing some stage of the magical liquid which, blended with this, that, the other of its companions, would create the port we know. Over the next hour or so, in an atmosphere combining lecture and social occasion, we went backwards and forwards in time. 'Try this 1920. Now, compare this 1940 with the 1980. This is only two years old – not legally port yet.'

It was dark as we began our tour of the enormous lodges, my host preceding me to flick a switch and cast a lonely pool of light as we penetrated deeper and deeper. There was a curious, solid silence around us, created by the floor of wood tiles and by the immense vats through which we threaded our way. A man could easily drown in one of them and they had a brooding, anthropomorphic presence, a veritable Hall of the Mountain Kings. In the farthest reach, locked away behind massive grills that really were cob-webbed, were the Methuselahs of the wine world – great barrels of port that had been lying there since the beginning of the century. All through the last years of Queen Victoria and the accession of Edward VII, through the Battle of the Somme and the Armistice, through the Depression, through the rise of Adolf Hitler, through Hiroshima, Bikini Atoll, the Korean War, the monsters had slumbered almost undisturbed, an impress-ive testimony to social stability. But it was only 'almost' undisturbed. 'We're continually drawing off a little – a very little at a time – to give body to new wine.'

And outside these cool, silent wooden caves was the oddest contrast of all – the bottling and packing plant. Bleakly modern – but stacked casually around in plastic crates like those that milkmen use – were dozens of very dirty bottles. They were the true vintage port – each with the little white dab of paint to show on which side it had been lying for fourteen years – brought here to be cleaned up, labelled, packed in wooden cases and sent to delight palates all round the world. Here, in this bright modern room was demonstrated the dynamism which had brought the Douro valley rail-way into being nearly a century ago and was now, alas, contributing to its decline, seduced, as we have all been seduced, by the ease and speed of road transport. 'Most of our wine now comes down to us by road tankers.'

The Portuguese Tourist Office, very much aware of the value of their little railway in generating much-needed tourist income, had gone out of their way to make my journey possible. In particular, they had provided me with three interpreters for three stages of the journey, three young women each of whom proved delightfully different from the other, but each of whom in her confidence and competence gave the lie to the comfortable Anglo-Saxon stereotype of the Latin woman as a cipher in a macho society. And each provided me, obliquely but therefore invaluably, with a view of her own country – and of mine.

So, on the first morning in Oporto, waiting for me in the hotel foyer was Manuela – crisp, attractive, encouragingly competent. Our first call was to be the railway station where a Very Important Railway Personage was to give me the historical and economic background of the little mountain railway, and arrange my itinerary. So we thought.

Outside the station a blind girl was singing, accompanied by a blind accordionist. She is well known in Oporto and, invariably, there is a crowd around her although she sings the same song over and over and over again. Her message is a warning to the emigrants who come through this gateway to the promised land:

> Do you really think you can achieve your dreams
> In some El Dorado far away?

The tune is harsh, hypnotic, plangent, infinitely melancholy. Supposedly, a people's songs give a clue to their soul but this contradicts – like the plangent *fado* of Lisbon – a people whose dominant characteristic seems, to an outsider, to be contentment. And yet, at a deeper level, the blind girl's song does indeed give a clue to the Portuguese character. The tune has an ululation, remote, barely detectable but indubitably there – the last faint sound of Africa. And one remembers the three different races that have moulded this country and its people. They are an Atlantic people: standing with Oporto behind you, there's nothing whatsoever but salt water between you and New York. But they are also heirs to a Mediterranean culture. And Africa ruled them for many, many years, not so long as in Spain but long enough to leave an ineradicable imprint.

We found that imprint again in the railway station. São Bento station is not very large, as modern stations go. It's built on the site of a convent, and there is still something ecclesiastical about the foyer. The proportions are not quite right so that it's like being at the bottom of a gigantic shoe box. But all is saved by those splendid murals which the Portuguese call *azulejos* and we translate, pedestrianly, as 'tiles'. In every town of Portugal they are to be found, sometimes cladding an entire building so it glints back in the sun in a riot of blue and green and gold. Sometimes, as at São Bento, they are pictorial – either multicoloured or in a universal blue. These in the station date from the 1930s and show a way of life which, in full flood at the time, is now rapidly departing: water-mills on the Douro, those graceful craft called *rebelos* which, before the coming of the railway, brought the wine down to Oporto. High up on the walls is a multicoloured series, grandiloquently showing the evolution of transport from prehistoric times down to the railway: tucked away in one corner is a picture of the first steam engine, now peacefully at rest in a museum.

Manuela and I set off in search of the Very Important Railway Personage, being directed and redirected down endless corridors, very high and narrow in the Portuguese manner, with incredibly high and narrow doors to match so that one felt rather like Alice in Wonderland after she had incautiously taken that drink. We ran the VIRP to earth at last in a room which, from my point of view, was a treasure house. The walls were covered with paintings, drawings, engravings, cuttings, cartoons, all devoted to the story of the railway. My mouth really did water, for here, in one room, was someone who would tell me all I wanted to know about the railway; there, seated at the desk, was the VIRP who would provide the key, and by my side was the highly competent translator through whom all this treasure would be transformed to my notebook.

So I thought.

There is a special technique for speaking through a translator which consists, in essence, of simply allowing the translator to translate. One should speak for only a minute or so – five minutes is the absolute maximum – then stop to allow the translation to be made. Socially, it's inclined to be a bit disconcerting: one has to stand with an air of modest intelligence and interest while the alien sounds fill the air. But it works – given that the speaker allows time for the translation to be made.

This the VIRP resolutely refused to do. He had a booming, resonant voice and for two and a half mortal hours that booming, resonant voice rolled on in an unstoppable wave. Manuela, as I found later, knew her stuff: not only was her command of idiomatic English perfect but she had the translator's technique of moving in during natural gaps so that the breaks seem less obvious. But she never had a chance. There were no natural gaps. The VIRP regarded any attempt at breaking in on his flow as an abrogation of his conversational rights, to be met with an irritated wave of the hand and a jacking up of the decibelic output. In vain I too attempted to stem the flood, dropping gradually all pretences of True Brit diffidence, pacing the room impatiently, interposing questions. I was simply ignored.

We had entered that room a little after 9 a.m. By 11.30 the luckless Manuela knew every detail (or, rather, every detail had passed through her head) relating to the entire Portuguese railway system from 11 May 1853, when Queen Joanna broke the first sod, down to about 1890. Which was where, brutally, I broke in, bellowing in a voice that rose even above the thunder: 'I'm not interested in the general system. I only want to know about the Corgo narrow gauge – the one where steam engines were running a year or so ago.'

He looked offended. 'Why do foreigners want to know about the bad things – about water-wheels and oxcarts and steam engines – instead of the good things?' At least, I assume that was what he said for Manuela's low-voiced translation was again swamped. Anyway, it would have been in

A passenger train, headed by a 1913 Henschel 4–6–0, runs through typical Douro Valley terrain near Regua. The trains are now pulled by diesels

vain to point out that tourists want to see oxcarts, not Ferguson tractors, water-mills not waterworks, because we, in industrialised societies, had been too clever by half and had cut off our roots. Over the next half-hour or so I tried to get some idea of the treasures displayed on the walls, but it was hopeless. Even when a question could be framed, the answer was an endless monologue with the subject buried within it beyond hope of exhumation.

I had given the whole thing up as a bad job, and was preparing to get myself out of the room when Manuela said, in a low voice, 'He says he will come with you.'

'What?!'

'He will come with you tomorrow. As far as Pinhao. To explain.'

I was appalled. But it would have been churlish to have refused – and anyway impossible to stop him travelling on his own railway. But my heart went out to the as yet unknown girl who would have an entire day of it.

The Northern Region of the Portuguese railway system conforms, exactly, with the riverine system of the Douro and its tributaries: in that mountainous country it would have been economically impossible to do otherwise. Thus the main, standard-gauge, track, which was begun in 1879, runs from Oporto along the northern bank of the river. A modern road accompanies it to Regua, some 80 kilometres from Oporto, but there the road cravenly

Two trains at Regua. On the left is the narrow-gauge-line train which runs up the Corgo line to Chaves. On the right the broad-gauge-line train from Oporto is about to continue up the Douro Valley

crosses to the southern bank and even today the railway is the only link for the little towns on the north bank beyond Regua, including Pinhao, the very heart of the wine district.

Running northward from this standard gauge are five narrow-gauge lines, each following the valley of a tributary of the Douro, and taking its name from it. Originally, it had been planned to link the five northern termini of the tributary lines in another line running parallel to the Douro but this plan fell through. One must either come back down the same line up which one travelled to the north, or take a bus across to the next terminus. I picked up the Corgo line, running from Regua to Chaves, partly because it passed through Vila Real, the capital of this whole extraordinary province of Tras-os-Montes, but mostly because it ended at the Roman town of Chaves. I have, in any case, got a thing about Rome and find it painful to pass up any Roman town, but there was a particular appropriateness in that Chaves, just ten kilometres short of the Spanish frontier, was on the Roman road running south – the direct ancestor of the little railway line. So, at 7.45 on a hot, bright October morning I left Oporto railway station, accompanied by the VIRP, Susanna the translator and some scores of assorted Portuguese, on the first leg of the journey. Susanna, incidentally, bore the name of one of the great port-producing families of the Douro – a name as familiar to the Portuguese as 'Sandeman's' or 'Cockburn's' is to the British – and so was able to provide a valuable – and vigorous – corrective to the idea that only the British really know about port.

The train comes momentarily back to the river just outside Oporto, giving one an unforgettable photo-flash of the gorge-like river, the two towering bridges built of seemingly delicate tracery and the golden city on each side. Then the train runs north in a great curve, before heading back to the river at Livraçao, the starting point of one of the tributary lines. The VIRP almost immediately collared Susanna and, feeling simultaneously guilty but relieved, I made my way back to the door. Portuguese railways have an alarmingly casual approach to safety, the exterior folding doors remaining open or closed according to the whim of the nearest passenger. I wondered how many passengers had been lost to the railway by an untimely precipitation through the open door, but it did give one a marvellously unrestricted view of the countryside.

The early morning mist disappeared, the golden sun shone upon endless rows of green and purple grapes, the land itself was green and fresh yet indubitably southern, an exhilarating combination. The train thundered on: after half an hour or so Susanna joined me, looking dazed, and after she, too, had united soul and body, we talked in that casual, inconsequential manner through which one learns far more of a strange country than during any set lecture. She gestured at a startling confection that swept by, a brand-new house, its walls colour-washed in eye-stunning pinks and yellows. 'Emigrants' houses,' she said scornfully. 'They come back to show off their wealth.' We talked of the famous wine that her grandparents produced and of the changes she had seen even in her short life. 'When I was a little girl, after the vintage, the pickers used to take bunches of artificial flowers to the lady of the house. They don't any more,' she said sadly. They used to have pretend bride-abduction: at Easter they burnt a figure of Judas: every village once would have its bull fight – harmless battles of will in which the beast was released unharmed. 'All gone, now.' Why? She shrugged.

'People leave; they travel away; times change.'

Suddenly there was a triumphant blast on the great klaxons and simultaneously the Douro came back into view, the Douro which would accompany us now for the rest of our journey on this train. The River of Gold seems to change its character almost every few yards. Here it is a narrow, deep channel down which the dark-green water rushes like a conduit: abruptly it becomes shallow and wide with the water chattering and sparkling. Elsewhere it is still, almost stagnant, with pools of scum at the water's

Six steam locomotives stand around the turntable at Regua

edge, or widening out into a deep still lake with the hills mirrored exactly within it. The stations are small, each with some local distinction: Ermida has a brilliant display of flowers, among them those superb, dark-blue convolvulus trumpets that light up the dreariest places – I've never seen them outside Portugal; Mosteiro has attractive formalised *azulejos* – but nothing to equal those at Pinhao.

We passed through Regua, en route to Pinhao, about 11 a.m. and there I undoubtedly owed a debt to the VIRP. We had returned to the carriage, and as the train came jolting across the junctions he leaned over and, grasping my arm, pointed. There, black in the sunlight and dignified even in death, were six immense steam locomotives. I don't suppose, on reflection, that they were particularly large but in this small station, among the nondescript diesels, they loomed like something from an heroic past. Later, the VIRP obtained permission for me to photograph them on my return from Pinhao, for which I was truly grateful; for this elephant's graveyard must surely be unique. One or two of them might, eventually, find a home in a museum – the Caminhos de Ferro has an excellent record in preserving historic material as I was to find – but most would remain here, gradually rusting away, for no part of them could conceivably be of use for any other purpose except to drive a steam locomotive. They looked like a relic not of the nineteenth century but medieval – Arthurian. One would not have been surprised to see Charlemagne going into battle on one. Or, better, Boadicea. What our Queen of the Iceni would have made of such chariots. . . .!

Pinhao, about half an hour down the line, was a delight, a flower-bright village that is the very centre and heart of the wine-producing district. It is here that the grape-pickers disembark, each group behind its drummer to walk two or three miles to one or other of the great quintas that cover the surrounding hills. There they will remain for about a fortnight, receiving food and lodging from the growers. It looks romantic work but it is hard. There is no shade on these naked hills, and as the sun rises the valley holds and traps the heat – one of the reasons why this is a successful wine-growing locality. Many of the pickers will have small farms of their own, but during this fortnight will be working for cash. But many, too, have come from the towns and cities – rather like the hop-pickers used to do in England before mechanisation killed their working holiday. Mechanisation has already entered many of the quintas for the crushing of the grapes. But the best are still done by foot for, by happy chance, the human body is of such a weight, and the human foot of such a dimension, as to break the skin without breaking the pips. This, too, is hard work: at the beginning of the session it is necessary to raise the legs high, as though one were climbing over a style, then thrust down. The treaders, men and women together, link arms and, to the single, monotonous thump of a drum, tread in unison for about two hours. They then break step and to lively accompaniment of accordion and drum – helped, too, by the juice they are treading but in an advanced and alcoholic form – literally dance in the must for another three or four hours. Much of what is produced will find its way as ordinary – if excellent – table wine to Portuguese tables: but some, too, will be lying in the cool lodges of the great international shippers ten, twenty, perhaps a hundred years from now.

The little station at Pinhao has a set of huge, superb *azulejos*, testimony at once of the importance of the village and the pride of the railway company that brought civilisation from the coast up to here. They tell the story of the locality – its topography, customs, work traditions – and are

Vineyards in the Douro Valley

beautifully executed but also so precise that Susanna was able to identify her grandparents' farmhouse. A band, trim in powder-blue uniforms with their splendid, glittering instruments at rest, were on the platform as our local train came in. Shortly afterwards, a long-distance train thundered in, the band struck up, elegantly dressed passengers descended, speeches were made and away we all went to an unknown destination.

I am quite unable to resist the lure of a band, following it as helplessly as any Hamelin child following the Pied Piper. Most of Pinhao seemed to have felt the same and some scores of us went along the village street to where the road bridge crossed the great river. One by one the villagers dropped away, leaving only the visitors and myself. The band tootled and thumped away, the sun shone, the river sparkled. On the far side of the river the informal procession turned into what was evidently private property: swept on by the band I entered with them. We passed down an

131

avenue lined with orange trees, their fruit still dark, glossy green, towards a little chapel and a clutter of white buildings. And as we approached them, the bells started ringing – and the sky exploded.

The Portuguese adore fireworks – not the timid, colourful things of other countries but great rockets that explode with a tremendous bang, telling the world far around what is happening. And what was happening here was the beginning of the vintage. The visitors were French, members of a wine confraternity, and this occasion that started with rockets and bells and more speeches would go on to include lunch. Why don't I join them, my informant said. I could see white-clothed tables under cool vines, jugs of wine, loaves of bread, and smell a most heavenly smell. The sun now stood immediately above the valley: behind me lay the long, hot walk back to the station, ahead lay coolness and, I would suspect, a first-class lunch. The temptation was almost overwhelming, but it would have been churlish to have left my companions without a thank-you or an explanation, for they were returning to Oporto by the next train. Reluctantly, I turned down the invitation. But I was still grateful to have been included, if only as a spectator, in a ceremony which was being repeated that day all over the wine-growing district – the beginning of the harvest, a ceremony which in one form or another would have been repeated annually ever since the Romans showed them how to grow grapes.

My companions and I separated at Regua. The little town has had a bad press. The kindest thing that travel-books can find to say about it is 'nondescript' or 'not particularly interesting'. In Oporto I was told it was little more than an extension of the railway station, the Clapham Junction of the Douro Valley. One would think it would be difficult for a town on the side of a great river, set among beautiful hills and laced with vineyards, to be unattractive but Regua really does do its best. It has succumbed to the twentieth-century scourge of urban sprawl, flinging out a mass of garages and flats and road bridges and little cafés to fill up every piece of level ground between river and hills. Back in the 1930s someone had vision, building a handsome balustrade high above the river in the town centre. They couldn't afford to build in marble or even the local granite, but used ferroconcrete much of which is falling apart. But the design was good, a row of balusters flanked at each end with a circular open space with a fountain in the middle. But the fountains are dry, one of the open spaces is given over to a lorry repair area with the obscene entrails of the monsters scattered greasily everywhere, and, at water level, a single immense dredger occupies the whole frontage. But away from the river, the town is lively enough with pleasant squares and comfortable cafés.

The narrow-gauge-line train standing at Regua station, about to journey up the Corgo line to Chaves

And it is the junction for the Corgo narrow-gauge-line, which I found by accident. I had descended from the high ground to the flat land bordering the river, attracted by a gipsy encampment. They had cheerfully gone back 10,000 years, their 'tents' nothing more than a piece of material thrown over a rickety frame and set in the midst of an indescribable rubbish dump. They ignored me, except to cuff a snarling cur from my path, and I went on down to where a stream – the Corgo – joined the Douro. A group of men were fishing up the stream – but what fishing. . . ! Nothing could more clearly show the richness of this land than their technique. One of them had a net – rather resembling that used by the retiarii in the Roman games – an immense but delicate looking fabric with weights all round its edge. Walking up the stream he would spot some sign quite invisible to me and, with a single graceful movement, throw the net. He never came up with less than half a dozen large fish in the net, any three of which would be a good meal: in less than half an hour's pleasant activity on a glorious Saturday evening he and his three companions had netted more than enough for their family's evening meal.

I followed them as they worked steadily upstream towards Pinhao and towards the mainline railway bridge that spanned the gorge, when I became aware of an extraordinary noise coming *down* the gorge – a rattling and a thumping and a clattering that sounded like a lot of mad little men talking to themselves. I looked up and there, high up on the right-hand bank of the gorge, was my train, *the* train, the narrow-gauge railway coming on down from Chaves to haven in Regua. It came steadily on, then swung in a curve on to the main line towards Regua just half a kilometre away, and I watched as it sailed across the bridge, still talking madly to itself. How did it do it? How did it join the standard gauge?

I just had to see, although the only way across the gorge was by a truly terrifying trestle bridge. A public footpath ran over it alongside the rails in the continental manner, but what with the drop on one side, and the river only too visible through the sleepers under foot, it was a singularly unpleasant crossing. But it was worth it in order to solve that problem. I don't quite know what I expected – rubber rails or an expanding and contracting bogey – but what I saw was an elegant solution to an engineering problem. The narrow gauge came down from the north, then swung westward to fit snugly *inside* the rails of the standard gauge like a child nestling in its mother's arms.

At ten o'clock the following morning I was on that little train as it clattered and chattered back over the bridge. There is something curiously timeless about Sunday travelling on railways, but I had not expected quite such a magical, wholly enchanted day. The train was drawn by an ordinary diesel but the carriages were old, very old: according to rumour they were part of Germany's reparation after World War I. Inside, they had a solid, curiously homely appearance, for they were entirely built of wood with sash windows that opened down to waist level. But it was the little observation platform that was, for a stranger, an unalloyed delight. It was, perhaps, four feet deep and running the width of the train – about eight feet – surrounded by a simple iron rail at waist height. Had the train been moving at speed then it would have been appallingly dangerous even in its heyday, for there was nothing to prevent the passenger being pitched over the rail: today, the danger was heightened by the fact that one of the two gates swung idly on its hinges, the catch long since broken so that every lurch of the train threatened to throw you clean out.

But the speed rarely rose to much more than 15 mph and, I would judge, was mostly around 12 mph. And at that speed, on this tiny platform in this narrow track, the passenger was virtually part of the countryside. The single track infiltrated rather than penetrated. Economy ensured that no width more than was absolutely essential would be cleared so that at times one was going through a green tunnel, at others the rock wall rose up at touching distance. The grass and flowers and herbs crept down on to the track, the little stations were simple bowers. Sometimes the track came to

Wooden carriage with observation platform

the very edge of a precipice so that one could look down and down and down to the endless ranks of vineyards and the workers among them, like so many bees even though this was a Sunday. The track wound violently backwards and forwards, taking advantage of every natural cutting and level so that the alien smell of the diesel was swept away and the perfume of the vast hillside rose like one unbelievable potpourri. Eucalyptus and pines, vines, olives, ferns, thyme, all combined in that bright, hot, but oddly bracing atmosphere. The road, which occasionally came into view, looked bleak and unwelcoming by contrast with that flower-decked, herb-strewn track.

It was with reluctance that I broke the journey at Vila Real about an hour up the line. The track lies on one side of an immense gorge – far more frightening than that outside Regua – on the other side of which Vila Real looks like a miniature Toledo. I found it a pleasant, but not outstanding town, lacking the raffish charm of Regua and the neatness of Chaves, but it

Steam locomotive and train running down the valley near Vila Real, past steep terraces of vineyards

seemed only courteous to pay my respects to the capital of Tras-os-Montes. 'Beyond the Mountains' is the official name of this province, romanticism breaking in even on bureaucracy, and it is the guardian of a way of life that is rapidly departing from Western Europe. Here is combined the best of north and south – southern vivacity and northern dependability, southern charm and northern cleanliness: a readiness to acknowledge the stranger, if that is what the stranger wants, but a refusal to swamp him with questions and unwanted hospitality. Change is breaking in, as Susanna, barely in her twenties, had sadly noticed. But there is an awareness of that fact, and among a few a conscious determination to exercise some control. Up further north, almost on the Spanish frontier, a village priest has set himself a crusade to bring back some of the older customs, or preserve those that remain. Some are, to say the least, dubious – such as a brutal version of the old nursery game 'Pin the tail on the donkey' where a blindfolded person has to find, and hit with a stick, a cockerel buried up to its neck in the earth. Others are more laudable, such as the restoration of the traditional ovens for baking bread which make excellent use of the sparse local fuel, and produce the most delicious bread.

Vila Real was wrapped in Sunday somnolence with the male population following that international custom of having a drink with friends – male

A Henschel 2–4–6OT four-cylinder compound Mallet, with Corgo line train, approaches Vila Real from Chaves

friends – while the little woman pursues her vocation at home in the kitchen. Even in this small and sleepy place on a Sunday I found an excellent restaurant, and afterwards continued a journey that had become even more dreamlike in the stillness of afternoon. *L'après-midi d'un faune* would have been an appropriate musical accompaniment – if one could have heard it above the chattering and the muttering, the clanking, banging, rattling of the train, a cacophony produced by the loose metal parts on the couplings and on the observation platforms.

After an hour's run we had climbed finally out of the rich valley, and were running on the bleaker plateau, the true 'land beyond the mountains'. The road became more visible: ominously, it was in a smart new livery of black and white, contrasting with the shabbiness of the train, and over long sections brand-new embankments had been created for it. Quite evidently, a lot of money was being spent on road transport. This little railway, whose timetable has remained unchanged since 1900, would have been closed when steam was abandoned five or six years ago, had it not been for a massive local outcry. But staff and crew run it still with a verve and dedication: at Regua, even on a Sunday, everyone, including the stationmaster, seemed to be on duty. And coming into Chaves, on the dot at 5.30, was like coming into harbour after an Atlantic crossing, the driver

An engine makes ready to leave Chaves station. Note the distinctive station architecture

greeting the first sight of the little town with a tremendous symphony on his klaxons. We'd made it – sixty kilometres in barely three hours.

Paradoxically, one has to travel north to go south for Chaves seems far more of a southern – a Mediterranean – town than any of the others I had seen from Oporto onwards. The Romans knew it as *Aquae Flaviae*: the town still draws a comfortable income from the spa that created it and the citizens still proudly refer to themselves as Flavians, not Chavese. It's a neat, clean, trim, bustling little town that just happens to possess one of the finest surviving Roman bridges and an exquisite little Renaissance square – odd things to find high up here in the lonely mountains. And yet, not so odd, for it marks the beginning of the Roman road south, and where the Romans went civilisation followed whether it's Northumbria or Tras-os-Montes. The sixteen-arch bridge crossing the Tamega looks good for another 1900 years or so: the paved road that runs over it continues on die-straight into the town, the very heart of the little place with cafés and shops lining it. It lost ground to the railway for fifty years or so – the line from Vila Real to Chaves was completed only in 1921 – but the whirligig of time is restoring its importance as that of the railway sinks, even though it is now cars and lorries, not the bronze legions of Rome, that move inexorably southward.

I had originally planned to take a bus to Bragança then return south by the Tua line, but to have done so would have meant leaving Chaves at dawn on the day after arrival, a discourtesy to such a town. In any case, I liked the idea of returning down by the same line, seeing, as it were, the other side of the pine-trees, the other view of the vineyard. There was a train at 11.15 and, after pottering round the little town, attended by my sprightly student interpreter, Carmen, I presented myself at the station at 11.05. To find that I had fallen victim to one of those maddening quirks that lie in wait for travellers.

The station-master himself was in the ticket office and, as soon as he saw me, said something reproachful. 'He has been waiting for you all morning,' Carmen translated. 'To show you the historic material.'

Historic material? Things clicked. On the journey up from Oporto the VIRP had said something about an historic collection at Chaves. I should have checked as soon as I had arrived but that numbness brought on by noisy movement had rendered me indifferent, on arrival, to anything but a hot bath and a long, long very cold drink. I apologised and explained.

The station-master ducked out of his little office and beckoned energetically. 'He wants you to go now. But we must hurry.'

We must, indeed: ten minutes to go and a treasure house to inspect. For this really was a treasure house, the genuine thing. Somehow, on arrival, I had missed seeing a long, grey shed with that magic phrase 'Historical Material' over its lintel. Railway lines led up to it. And stopped.

The Regua train was waiting by the platform, crowded, the diesel already throbbing. 'Hurry. Hurry.' And at that, we threw dignity to the winds, the three of us running to the shed, Carmen between the two of us breathlessly translating apologies, reproaches, explanations. The station-master threw the great doors open and there they stood, two beautiful, gleaming steam locomotives, resplendent in their livery of black and dark red and brilliant brass, looking as though they were ready to go through those doors, down those lines and take up the duties they had abandoned five years ago when the faceless, anonymous diesels had taken over this line. Beside them was a delightful little bogey of a kind I had only ever seen in early Hollywood comedies – the kind of thing on which Fatty Arbuckle or Charlie Chaplin is pumping for dear life while pursued by villains in a train. In a little room behind were more treasures – pictures, lamps, posters. We swept round almost at a run. I could have wept. The station-master could have wept. Carmen, I don't doubt, could have wept.

But Chronos, the inexorable compiler of timetables, was against delay – or so I thought at the time. The next train was not until 2.30: if it arrived in even twenty minutes late I would miss the connection for Oporto. Which would mean I would miss my flight to Lisbon, and so on in the escalation of modern transport. I had, as I was to discover, done the little railway a grave injustice but I was not to know that at the time and so, as the klaxon sounded impatiently, I took my place on the observation platform and the train moved out.

I had bought bread and wine, olives and grapes, the perfect traveller's meal, and set them out gratefully on the wooden seat opposite. Then I went through the usual ritual, checking papers. Money? Yes. Guide books and bumf generally? Yes. Air ticket? Yes. Passport?

Passport . . . It wasn't lost, I knew exactly where it was: in the safe of some hotel between Chaves and Oporto. It was not the standard passport, but what is known as a Visitor's passport. My own had just gone out of date and would have taken two or three weeks to renew. However, for some reason best known only to the mandarins of the Foreign Office, one can get this substitute within half an hour over a post office counter. It is not, however, the substantial dark blue passport, last evidence of the British Empire, which could be mistaken for nothing else, but a nasty little piece of buff cardboard which could be mistaken for almost anything else. The hotelier of wherever had faithfully passed over the mass of other papers but reposing in his safe now was that nasty little bit of buff cardboard.

The bright day grew dark: the smooth, cool wine of Chaves turned to vinegar as I contemplated my immediate future. I thought of Ernest Bevin, our first Foreign Secretary after World War II, not the greatest of Foreign Secretaries, but one who roundly enunciated his essential policy – to be able 'to go down to Victoria Station, buy a railway ticket, and go where the hell I liked without a passport.' Poor Ernie: forty years afterwards and we are no nearer that ideal as the resigned queues shuffling up to passport controls bear testimony.

And here was I passportless. Stateless. I conjured up the vision of cold-eyed Portuguese officials, inspecting me for the wrong shade of political opinion: of cold-eyed British officials, inspecting me for the wrong shade of skin pigmentation, neither liking what they saw and sending me back to the other, condemning me, forever, to eat airline food five miles up in the air – a fate Zeus would have hesitated to have inflicted on Prometheus.

But there was a certain comfort in the situation: there was nothing, whatsoever, I could do about it now. In Oporto, perhaps, or Lisbon I would

Two trains pass at Vidago station on the Corgo line. On the right is the Chaves to Regua and on the left the 7.05 from Regua

have to start talking. But now – the sun was shining, the wine was not after all vinegar, the bread superb.

The little train was already full and became ever fuller with each stop: people with enormous bundles; farmers taking a sack of maize to a slightly better market; mamas going to visit married daughters; young men off to the big city of Vila Real – all the manifold reasons why people travel here displayed. I stood again on the platform, drinking my wine, and a young man joined me, as we racketed along.

'You like the vapour machines?' he said in careful English.

'?'

'The vapour machines: the material historical.'

'Ah, yes. The steam engines.'

'They are beautiful, are they not?' He was an engineering student from Lisbon, returning from holiday. He spoke of the days of steam as of Paradise Lost. 'It was like the Wild West. I go to see them every time I go to Chaves.'

We fell to talking about the past of the railway. It is difficult to emphasise how important a role it played in the social life of the locals. Much of

Portugal is at least a generation behind the rest of Western Europe. Twenty years ago some thirteen per cent of the population lived in villages quite inaccessible by road: as late as the 1920s some of the roads even near Lisbon were quite impassable in winter. Here, in Tras-os-Montes, the little narrow-gauge railway was quite literally a lifeline, discharging the same function in the 1950s as the railway system discharged in Britain in the 1850s – that is, bringing people together and opening up markets to them. It was so important that it became something of a political football. Most of the system was publicly owned until the 1930s when the Salazar regime transferred it to private ownership. It has again become publicly owned but, in the meantime, the road has emerged as a formidable rival. 'It takes me twenty-four hours to get to Lisbon by train,' the student said, 'I can do it in twelve by coach – leaving in the morning and getting in at evening – and, of course, it is much more comfortable.' I saw his point. It was delightful now, on a hot bright afternoon. But on a black December day, these wooden carriages without heating or upholstery and draughts at every side must be penitential cells. 'But I always travel by rail when I go on holiday.'

And on we rattled through that wild, sunlit, lovely landscape, with the smell of that vast potpourri again around us, through Pedras Salgadas, through Vila Real, through Escariz, through half a dozen tiny stations unknown except to those who ascended and descended, until we came again to Regua. And reality. My problems returned in all their blackness at the sight of the train to Oporto, waiting impatiently for us.

But I had counted without the blissful efficiency of the Portuguese Tourist Office, the blissful humanity of the little Corgo Railway. As I hurried towards the Oporto train a figure came dashing up – the Regua station-master. 'Mister Chambley. Passport.' That was the extent of his English. My Portuguese ran to perhaps half a dozen more words. We stood looking helplessly at each other, then he took my arm, forcibly taking me away from the Oporto train to his tiny office. It was crowded and very noisy and somebody thrust a phone into my hands. There was a distant gabble of Portuguese in which the words 'Chaves' and 'Passport' dominated. I gabbled back in English in which the words 'Oh God. Oporto' dominated. Nobody was getting any further. Outside came the triumphant double blare of the klaxons of the Oporto diesel. In an agony of frustration and indecision I passed the phone back to the station-master. He, too, gabbled for some time in Portuguese and then, with admirable restraint, wrote down two magical sentences on a piece of paper, pointing vigorously down:

16.30 Passport
17.00 Pôrto

Even I could understand that the passport was on its way from Chaves, would arrive here at 16.30 and there was a train to Oporto half an hour later. The hotelier must have taken my passport to the Tourist Office and they, with considerable initiative, had taken the chance that I could be stopped at Regua and sent the passport on by train.

And so it worked out, for I had done the little Corgo Railway an injustice. At precisely 16.25 the gallant little train, still madly muttering to itself, clacked into view; at 16.30 the diesel sank to rest with a great sigh. At 16.31 or thereabouts an envelope was thrust into my hand. I again existed.

The mainline train seemed enormous, like a Cunard liner after a Channel ferry. There were washing facilities and cold beer and upholstered seats. But there was no longer the feeling of being part of the landscape through which one was passing, no longer the friendly chattering. Only the deep, solemn thunder of the great diesels, hurling the hundreds of tons of metal and humanity through the darkening evening down the River of Gold, on to Oporto and the Atlantic and the world beyond.

INDIA
Line of Dreams
PETER HILLMORE
Based on a film directed by Gerry Troyna

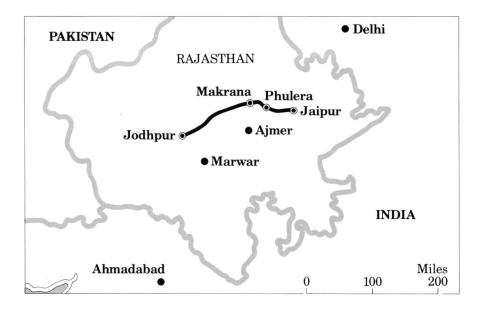

Of all the famous trains on which I have had the opportunity to travel –
from the Train Bleu to the Orient Express, from the Golden Arrow to the
Tokyo Bullet – none has fascinated me as much as any single train in
India. There, be it on the Grand Trunk route, or in the magical-sounding
Teagarden Express, or merely on a small, nondescript stopping-train from
nowhere in particular to nowhere much else, I am a convert to trains, a
devotee of this inimitable form of travel. I still treasure my subscription to
Newman's *Indian Bradshaw*: seventy-six rupees, 'post free per ordinary
post', 'a complete guide for railway and airway travellers, containing
specially arranged time and fare tables for all railways . . . and places of
tourist interest in India'. Once I've picked my copy up, it's hard to put it
down again. (But travellers should note that the Bombay–Delhi express
now leaves from Queen Victoria five minutes earlier than it did two years
ago. . . .)

Why Indian trains particularly? As with the best love affairs, I can re-member the precise moment when interest and affection turned to passion, and it was on this very route. The train had left Jodhpur about an hour before, more or less on time, and I was settled drowsily in my seat. The whirring fan was trying in vain to relieve the fierce heat. Outside the window the never-ceasing movement of India continued, as people went about their lives with infinite patience, with the same air of resignation and fatalism as the oxen they tended. A woman was silhouetted against the sky, her dark sari rippling gently, a water bottle balanced on her head with classic and timeless grace. Beyond her stretched the vast continent of India, horizon after horizon. As I gazed at this scene, half idly, but half painfully aware that a European will always be a stranger in this country, no matter how long he spends here, no matter how much of the culture he absorbs, or how sympathetic he becomes, the little steam engine suddenly gave a piercing whistle, plaintive and defiant. A shiver of pleasure ran through me, and the instant somehow became transfixed in my memory, to be recalled now whenever India is mentioned. That moment on the 'Line of Dreams' was the moment when, as Paul Scott writes of a character in one of his novels, I 'discovered the scent behind the smell', and from then on the scent of India was inextricably mingled with the smell of her trains.

The metre-gauge line that covers the 250 miles between the two ancient capitals of Jodhpur and Jaipur is an insignificant stretch on the great rail-way map of India. The British laid the foundations of what became the most extensive railway network in Asia. The first tract, a twenty-five-mile stretch between Bombay and Thana, opened in 1853; by 1869 there were about 4500 miles of line, and the main workshops of the East India Railway had already opened at Jamalpur in 1862. Many of the lines and trains are more celebrated than the Marudhar Express – those of Darjeeling and of Simla, for instance, or the Nilgiri Express, that goes up and down the mountains from 'Ooty' to Mettapaylayam in the south. But no Indian journey is unremarkable.

In an essay called 'The Dreamlike World of India', Jung described as an Indian archetype the very experience a Westerner may recognise on an Indian train: 'It is quite possible that India is the real world, and that the white man lives in a madhouse of abstractions . . . life in India has not yet withdrawn into the capsule of the head. It is still the whole body that lives. No wonder the European feels dreamlike: the complete life of India is something he feels dreamlike about. . . .'

Certainly the whole body of India lives on the train. From the first class to the third, via second class, and sometimes something called 'intermediate' class (and including even luxury private coaches tagged on to the end of the train for groups of Europeans who wish to keep themselves apart from the dreamlike state of India), literally all human life is here.

According to official statistics, a staggering 25,000 million journeys were made on the trains in 1980. And that was just the number of people who bought tickets. Add to that the countless number hanging on the side of the carriages or perching precariously on the roofs for even the longest and most arduous journeys, and the total must surely be doubled. A train in India never, or only very rarely, departs less than totally full. From early morning, or even the night before, passengers queue for the privilege of buying a ticket. Some will stand patiently in one line for hours, only to be told they should be in another. There are queues for trains running several days hence, and many of these trains too will already be full. Sometimes the authorities try to be helpful and put up little coloured lights above the train routes to signify the availability of seats. This would indeed be helpful, but unfortunately they sometimes forget to adjust the lights from day to day.

Above the ticket office at Jodhpur a large sign warns the long queues, in that comprehensible yet strange English that makes you feel slightly disorientated, or as if you yourself have somehow dropped back in time: 'Punctuality. Every attention is paid to ensure punctuality as far as is practicable, but the administration give notice that they do not undertake that the train will start or arrive at the time specified in the timetable. The right to stop the train at any station on the line, although not marked as a stopping station, is reserved.' And so it will prove.

A station in India is always much more than the starting point of a journey; like some medieval church in England, it's the place to meet, to loiter, to sell, to steal, to gossip, even to sleep. Victorian passengers used to complain that trains seemed to stop at stations for the sole purpose of allowing the train crew and passengers to chat to the locals on the platform, and even today that seems to be a prime reason at many stations. But should you be so foolish as to complain about the meandering nature of an Indian train, a Railway Board official will at once, and proudly, produce statistics to show that over eighty per cent of the trains run on time every year. There doesn't seem to be much point in replying that you must have travelled on the other twenty per cent, or in pointing out that journey times on all but the great expresses have hardly changed since 1910, or that the average speed of Indian trains is only twenty-three miles an hour. . . .

It is likely that even those clutching tickets will not necessarily be

Indians sit at sadhus' shrine to Lord Shiva in front of Jodhpur station

guaranteed a place on this afternoon's train, however punctual, for it looks
overbooked. We first-class passengers, a pampered lot, hover nervously; if
all goes to plan and according to regulations, there should be a list hanging outside each first-class coach, with seats allotted to our names, but
experience has taught us that these lists are not always as complete as we
could wish. Meanwhile we resort to the 'Railway Retiring Room' – for us a
'Waiting Room for First Class Gents' – where passengers (first class) may
not only wait, but can also book rooms to sleep, or wash, or at least escape
from the fierce dry heat and busy life of the platform. Outside, the more
modest travellers squat with their cooking pots and provisions wrapped in
lengths of brightly coloured cloth. The bundles, carefully tied, lie on the
platform like soft and shapeless sculptures. And everywhere move the
licensed vendors of snacks for hungry and thirsty travellers, selling, for

instance, amongst a great variety of wares, bright green bananas, mangoes, a choice of exotic sweets (puri and guub jaman), or even an Indian version of Coca-Cola, known as 'Thumbs-Up'.

The station at Jodhpur is like thousands of stations all over India, quite ordinary, with aluminium roofs covering the platforms and the huge, teeming booking office. Even the smallest station in India is not really small: the minimum platform length, established over a century ago, is no less than 600 feet. (The world's longest platform, for people who collect such statistics, is at Sonepur in India, and is 2415 feet.) The most important stations are immense and impressive. Some, such as Lahore, were deliberately built like fortresses, complete with bomb-proof towers and heavy doors which could seal off the inside of the station. Queen Victoria station in Bombay, designed as a curious blend of Victorian and Venetian Gothic with a profusion of Indo-Islamic thrown in, is unique. Known simply as 'VT', it makes St Pancras (on which it was modelled) look like a country halt and the Victoria and Albert Museum like a simple cottage.

Jodhpur station never set out to rival 'VT', but there was a time when its own ambitions were nevertheless clear. The stretch of line between Jodhpur and Jaipur was originally the personal property of, and the link between, two great ruling families of Maharajahs, and a symbol of their power and authority. The Maharajah of Jodhpur not only had his own carriage of sumptuous proportions (the present first-class carriages are in fact the former second-class ones; the original first-class carriages had separate adjoining compartments for the servants of the passengers), his coach even had a throne in it. At Jaipur there is still an enormous building of carved pink stone at the end of a small siding in the station. This is the Viman Bhawan, the alighting place for members of the royal family of Jaipur and their important guests. Next to the special platform are suites of rooms complete with baths, so that distinguished travellers could wash and change, and emerge from the station looking as if they had never been travelling. When the Queen of England alights at Victoria, she steps on to a red carpet, but has to wait until she gets home for a wash and brush-up.

Although the railways of India were conceived as one Great Design, they were by no means built to a single plan. Decisions were made and investors sought thousands of miles away in England; the initial plans were governed by economic criteria – the need to shift Indian exports, such as cotton, to England – and military requirements such as troop movements. The railways were built by private capital under Government guarantees, so profitability was at least as important a consideration as the local social needs a line might serve. Then too there was the added complication that India was a collection of independent states, governed by a mass of powerful ruling families. In the state of Rajasthan alone, the area which embraces both Jodhpur and Jaipur, there are twenty-six Maharajahs, with countless relations (in the whole of India there are about five hundred Maharajahs), and even since Independence these families have retained their special status. Before the British arrived, their power had been absolute, and even after the British had come, their influence persisted as the policies laid down by the conquerors had to be formulated and carried out with their co-operation.

The Maharajah of Jodhpur required a railway station before the Great Design in London had ordained one for his state, so he built it himself, drawing on the huge funds in his exchequer that in turn were raised from the villagers. His motive was partly economic: the work involved would provide employment for thousands of his people (a later Maharajah used this argument less worthily to justify the building of a huge palace as a Famine Relief project!), and partly opportunist, in that he shrewdly assumed that it would give Jodhpur a great importance on the route between Bombay and Delhi. As indeed it did: at one time, before Partition, the line went as far as Karachi and made Jodhpur that ultimate status symbol in railway hierarchy – a Junction. But the Maharajah also built his line because in the middle of the last century technology itself was the ultimate status symbol, a sign of Progress. The line from Jodhpur was there long before there were trains to run on it, and for about forty years the rail traffic was pulled, not by engines puffing clouds of black steam, but by stolid horse or bullock power.

Today the line no longer belongs to the ruling family of Jodhpur, but has been absorbed by the less magnificent Railways Board; its employees (some of the five million employees of the Board) are no longer servants of a ruler who until only a few years ago could cause a train to depart earlier or later than schedule to suit himself. But the train is still the best direct way to the state capital of Jaipur and indeed, unless you are rich enough to fly, there is no other way to cross the great plain and salt lakes. The airport that the previous Maharajah developed from a desert strip to full international status is now used only as a training centre for the Air Force, apart from a few expensive domestic flights, mainly for tourists.

Most of my fellow passengers on the Marudhar Express are bound for Jaipur, though some will get off at the marble centre of Makrana, and a few at other small stops along the line. But nearly everyone, including large numbers who left the Bombay–Delhi train to join this one, will sit for six hours until we reach the 'pink city', the state capital, and the final stopping point of the Express. Normally the station staff at Jodhpur is unexcited by the arrival and departure of the train, but today, for some reason, things are different. The crowds of travellers who have shinned on to the carriage roofs, hoping to travel free, are being cleared off. First they are asked to leave by a policeman; when that fails, a second policeman uses a long stick to reinforce his entreaties. The displaced travellers attempt to cram themselves into the already overcrowded carriages, at least until the train departs and they can climb back on to the roof. The momentarily abandoned roof is being swept, and the little steam train is covered with flowers. This can hardly be in honour of my Press Card and the 'dear old *Observer*' – as the station-master of Ootacamund once fondly referred to it – and sure enough, I am told by a porter in a bright-red official turban that a Very Important Person is travelling on the train today – the Magistrate. He must above all be given 'a good impression of the train', though where he is going and why he is so important the porter cannot tell me.

On the move at last, in the train two carriages down from mine I fall into conversation with a real Maharajah. Well, not quite. His name is Maharajah Swarup Singh, and he is 'only' the uncle of the present Maharajah of Jodhpur. He is not wearing the riding breeches to which his city gave its name, but there is no doubt he is different from the ordinary run of passenger. I had already noticed him on the station, sitting apart from the other travellers, and accepting a glass of water from the waiting-room attendant with a gesture that was at once courteous and arrogant. Few people refer to him by his title now, but railway officials still call him 'your highness', even though he has had to pay for his ticket and no longer has the authority to advance the departure of the train. Although he tells me that the title which gives him the greatest status nowadays is the letters he can put after his name – Ex.MLA, a former member of the Assembly – Swarup Singh can recite the genealogy of his family with an assurance that would make even Sir Iain Moncreiffe blink: 'My family goes back, originally, to 1212 although the first gentleman was supposed to be the 136th generation from another area. In 1212 they came to this part of the country and from then on we were fighting around Jodhpur, so if you look around the area you will find a lot of castles and forts all established because we arrived in the area gradually and had to build up our power bases.'

Almost every Indian you speak to has a curiously disembodied sense of time, spanning centuries as if they were months. In Makrana, for instance, I met the local employer of the marble workers who told me that his family

Signalman with flags on the
Marudhar Express

Swarup Singh plays polo – on a bicycle

had been in charge 'only since 1600'; now Swarup Singh, Ex.MLA, remarks that the forts at Jodhpur 'were built in 1459 and in due course, right up to 1952, we were breaking down and rebuilding the walls'.

He can remember the times when it took more than just a magistrate to impress the passengers and the railway staff enough to decorate the train. For centuries – or was it just weeks? – the rulers of Jodhpur and Jaipur were constantly at war and only strategic marriages between the two families would bring about an uneasy peace and joyous celebration. And when the railway came, the celebrations took to the tracks. Swarup Singh recalls the last great union between the two houses, when there was indeed nothing slower than a Jodhpur train: the whole track was lined with torches as the marriage procession made its way down the line, stopping at almost every place en route for feasting and dancing. No one has any idea how long the journey took, but it was the last time the train was indeed a Royal Train. Now, like Swarup Singh, it is stripped of its royal titles. And now, like the train, Swarup Singh lives out a pastiche of royal splendour. He still plays polo, like his ancestors, but a different kind of polo – on bicycles, which gives the game a surrealist air. He still talks of fierce battles between two ruling houses – but they are battles fought out on the playing fields of Mayo, his Indian public school.

While we talk, the train has been crossing the vast Thaar desert, the 'Land of Death', as it is called, and from which, according to some scholars, the name of Jodhpur derives. Rajasthan (formerly Rajputana) means 'Abode of Kings', and the state is the ancient territory of the Rajputs, a proud race of warriors whose turbulent history – long preceding that of the family of Swarup Singh – is full of stories of men and women who followed unquestioningly the Rajput code, very much like the Samurai of Japan or the medieval knights of Europe. The Rajputs worshipped the horse Aswa, and the sword Asi, which some say gave its name to Asia.

In this land, drought and famine are facts of life, said to be the result of a curse laid on Jodhpur at the time of its foundation in the fifteenth century. The story runs that a hermit who lived in a pleasant site by a waterfall was harshly interrupted in his meditations, and ordered by the Maharajah's soldiers to move away, since a fort was to be built on this spot. The hermit roundly cursed them and the Maharajah, and said that from then on nothing would grow and prosper there. The Maharajah was naturally perturbed on learning that a holy man had laid a curse on his city before the first stones had even been laid; he apologised, in an attempt to placate the hermit, and with some success. The holy man could not lift a curse once made; all he could do was to modify it, so that the famine would fall only every third year. To this day, it may be a coincidence, but there is no rain every third year, and precious little in the years between.

'This year the situation is very serious,' Swarup Singh points out to me. 'You see, the green grass is growing all around, but there is no seed in it . . . it is the green famine, as I call it. . . . A man can survive by walking and using his brains, but the animals find it difficult to survive this arid zone of ours.'

But the curse is not among the many practical reasons the people leave on the trains from Jodhpur, passing out of the town with its six-mile wall and seven gates. In India people have learnt to live with the gravest of misfortunes; the local paper prints lists of how many villages are without water as automatically as an English paper will record the county cricket scores. At this time of year, already there are reports that over a hundred people have died of exposure in the intense heat of the Rajasthan summer.

Leaving Swarup Singh to sip his tea in the comfortable first-class compartment, I fell into conversation with the chief inspector of tickets, as curious and cryptic a character as his name, O.P. Dixit, seems to suggest. A man of secrets, a detective, a hunter of men – of men, in this case, who have not bought tickets to travel on the Marudhar Express. With remorseless cunning, O.P. Dixit tracks down the fare dodgers, to whom even the low fare of seven rupees is much more than a day's wages (always assuming they are lucky enough to have work), and who travel, moving from carriage to carriage, from roof-top to roof-top. As astonishing and resourceful an official as you will ever meet, O.P. Dixit is no quaint type out of an H.R. Keating Indian detective story, but rather a menacing and cynical figure, more at home in a Raymond Chandler novel:

'It was one of those days when the sun was hotter than Raja's curry. The noise of the train hammered in my head like the drum of a Hindu temple, and the steam drenched me like the sweat on a European's brow. And then I spotted the lurking figure of a fare dodger. . . .'

O.P. can tell, so he says, a fare dodger the minute he walks into a carriage to check the tickets: 'It is the eyes that give them away. They look shifty at the sight of my uniform, they look away, and then they run away. I chase them down the train. It is my job to save the railways' revenue and I will not give up. Many times I have been rewarded for my detective work by the authorities.'

But he knows there is more to uncovering what he calls 'ticketless travelling' than just walking into a compartment in an official uniform with shiny buttons and a ticket punch. They are a cunning, even violent, lot, these fare dodgers, and so he must use cunning, if not violence, to catch them. And so O.P., carrying his enthusiasm for his job to extraordinary lengths, has become a master of disguise. Disappearing into the lavatory in his uniform, he will emerge a short while later every inch a beggar, naked but for a loincloth, a farmer with grubby hands and worn clothes, a holy man with garlands and incense, or – if he is to patrol the first-class section – a portly businessman. He keeps his wardrobe in a bag, ready to change costume as occasion demands.

O.P. Dixit at his retirement party

Normally he sports a shaggy nineteenth-century Russian peasant's beard, but he thinks nothing of shaving this off in the course of duty, to appear in his most successful role, that of a woman. A little more preparation, a little more time in the lavatory, and let the ticketless travellers beware! Perhaps I look a little sceptical as he boasts of being the greatest drag artist on the railways, the Danny La Rue of Jodhpur, for he insists on showing me his personal album, full of photographs of himself in his numerous disguises. I am impressed and convinced. In not one of them does O.P. Dixit look like O.P. Dixit. But he confides that the date of his retirement is imminent, decreed by some official hundreds of miles away in Delhi, who is obviously oblivious of the legend he has become among the staff and travellers on this route.

We part in the corridor, and I don't see him again on the train – or at least, I don't *think* I saw him again . . . one scruffily dressed peasant gave me a broad smile and something that could have been a wink . . . I see him finally when we arrive at Jaipur, once more in his official uniform, and wearing a satisfied smile. It has been a good journey for him, but for every ticketless traveller caught there is now 'much paperwork' to be done, as well as the minutiae of recording the legitimate farepayers, like myself. He went off towards the office, dreaming nowadays not of the big arrest, the catch that will make future generations of inspectors revere his name, so much as whether his superiors in Delhi will somehow decide to postpone

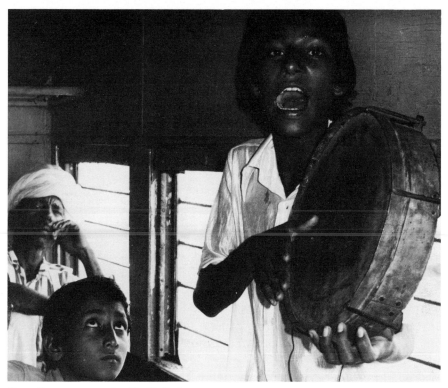

Travellers are entertained by Kailash

his forced retirement, and allow him to patrol the Marudhar Express for years to come.

But alas, I heard later that they did not relent, and O.P. Dixit has since retired, with great ceremony and formal leave-taking, to cherish his dreams and photographs.

I at least have no qualms about colliding with the ticket inspector. For a European the fares are laughably cheap (especially if you have a green 'India Rail' pass, granting unlimited travel). But it would be a disaster for young Kailash, one of the ticketless travellers whom O.P. Dixit regularly tracks the length of the train. Kailash is a twelve-year-old boy, but he is not one of your typical fare dodgers. The train is as much his source of employment as it is O.P. Dixit's, if less sanctioned by officialdom, for Kailash travels backwards and forwards between Jodhpur and Jaipur, earning his living as a singer. His slight frame has several scars acquired while jumping from car to car, or hanging on like a monkey to the outside of the coaches as the inspector goes by. Sometimes, if O.P. Dixit gets too close, Kailash might have to change his route by getting off at Makrana (the town that once provided the marble for the Taj Mahal, and now for the fireplaces of middle-class homes in Delhi, Bombay and Madras). Or perhaps he may simply change trains at Phulera, the largest marshalling yard on the whole metre-gauge network.

On this particular day, Kailash too is having a good journey. By the time I meet him his singing has already landed a few rupees in his tambourine. Once he is confident that I am not a new undercover agent for the Railways Board, he is willing to tell me his rather sad and hard life story for a few rupees more. Perhaps his responsibilities, heavy for a twelve-year-old boy, add to the plaintive tone in his pure voice, as he sings in the strange tonal scale of Hindu pop songs. For Kailash already has a child-wife back in Jodhpur, whom he must support though he has not yet been allowed to meet her. Helped by a friend of his who speaks better English, he tells me a complicated tale of his family, full of deaths and perennial hardships, and broken only by exceptional days when he earns as much as thirty rupees to take home to his mother. But some days he may earn nothing, or as little as five rupees. Some of his scars, he says, are the result of fights with passengers who have asked him for specific songs, and then refused to pay, knowing there is no one to whom he can complain.

Kailash will probably go to the cinema (one rupee) before returning to Jodhpur, both because every young Indian boy goes to the cinema as often as possible to see the extraordinary films, where the hero continually bursts into song as he swings from chandeliers or thumps the villain (but never gets to kiss the girl), and also because he has to top up his repertoire with the latest songs. I see him too for the last time on Jaipur station, with a group of his friends, perhaps just off to the cinema. He had decided not to busk in our first-class section of the train, perhaps because he felt it was too risky, or his experienced eye told him that the pickings would not justify the risk. Besides, on this occasion he had already had the money I had paid him for his own story, one that must in the end always remain outside the European's proper understanding. However long I talk to Kailash, no matter how friendly we become amid the passing bustle and camaraderie of the journey, we will always be strangers on a train.

It is sometimes said that the great contributions of the British to India were the language, the railways and the civil service. All three come together on an Indian train, even on a relatively unimportant line like this. But the railways are bureaucracy gone mad. Of the five million people employed by the Board, it seems as if four and a half million of them are involved in filling out forms. 'An overnight journey?' Then of course you need bedding. Please fill in these three forms, promising to submit

Trays with drinks are passed into the carriages

yourself to unspeakable penalties should you fail to return a sheet. (Five minutes before the train leaves, there is no sign of the bedding. Four minutes, and three officials come down the platform. Two of them are carrying the bedding – freshly laundered – and the third is clutching yet another form, committing one to further penalties. But in all my train journeys I have never failed to acquire my bedding, minutes before the train left.)

'You are hungry?' Then you will need a meal, so let bureaucracy lend a hand in its all-helpful way. Some trains have restaurant cars (and of course on every station you can buy all manner of drinks and spicy foods: the gourmets on the train can tell you which station has the best tea, which platform the best samosas, and who to buy fruit from). Before Station A an inspector will ask you whether you want Western, meat, or vegetarian for lunch. (On no account ask for Western, for it is nothing but limp, stale sandwiches, even worse than British Rail can provide; meat is risky; vegetarian is delicious.) At Station A, the conductor will telegraph ahead to Station B, where the assorted tin trays will be loaded aboard, to be consumed, and taken away again at Station C. It does not bear thinking how many tin trays are in transit across India at any one time.

But for many, bureaucracy was what made this train the Line of Dreams. By the time we had reached Phulera, passing the half-forgotten tombs of

Vultures fly over the shrines at Asop

long-forgotten rulers, landmarks in the bloody history of Rajasthan, I was glad to get out and stretch my legs, and buy some of the bread that other travellers said was the best on the whole route. During the wait I gossiped, as is the custom, with a stranger on the platform. He introduced himself as Mr Mandis, a retired engine driver, now in his eightieth year, who refuses all offers of rides on the footplate because of the stirring memories it would bring back. For him, and thousands, millions, like him, the bureaucracy of the railways brought relief from an all-pervasive, more inbuilt form of bureaucracy endemic in Indian life, that of the caste system, which kept a man to a regulated and possibly lowly status laid down thousands of years ago. With the coming of the railways, skill became a form of status, lessening the tyranny of caste, and bringing the freedom of a regular wage.

In his dated English slang, Mr Mandis reminisces of a time when engine drivers were the élite of the country, the very manifestation of Progress. Railway workers had regular uniforms, and comfortable accommodation in surprisingly grand buildings in the stations. Mr Mandis is an Anglo-Indian (or rather, a South American Indian), and he and a few others struggle to keep that other legacy of the British, Christianity, alive in the region. They collect enough money to pay a priest to visit the dusty old church at Phulera, yet another symbol of a half-forgotten period of Indian history. But with a congregation of at the most fifteen, the biggest problem, he tells me sadly, is money, or rather the lack of it:

'It used to be so different. In the olden days, you couldn't get into the church on a Sunday. The whole jing bang would come to worship: passengers, train drivers, everyone. . . . We could afford to buy what we wanted in the markets. I had servants and after I got my certificate, I had people working under me and I used to buy them a new uniform every year. Oh yes, we were élite.'

The drivers are still an élite, but Mr Mandis does not want to hear that. They are irresponsible youths who have no idea how things used to be. As the train leaves Phulera, I can see him waving gently through the steam, before he turns and goes back to his lonely house, perhaps stopping on the way to light a solitary candle in the church. For him 'there is no jollification in the station' now.

As the train strains up a moderately steep incline, the engine roars louder, and belches out clouds of steam. There was a time when the Maharajah's train was spoken of with great pride wherever railways were discussed, and it was notable for being the first line to have electric lighting in the carriages. Later people began to say ruefully that there was nothing so slow as a Jodhpur train, but that seems a little unfair now, as it covers the journey to Jaipur a lot faster than other trains travel in India.

We pass still more old tombs, which would look spectacular if they were the first we had seen on our arrival in India, but which we now rank among commonplace marvels. The land that has succeeded to the part that fell under the hermit's curse is nevertheless still bare and barren. There are large tracts of green, but 'the green famine' persists, and the animals still scratch disconsolately at the ground. The villages cluster close to the railway tracks, as if the prosperity represented by the train will somehow rub off on them. Children wave at the train as it passes; occasionally women stop their never-ending work to gaze after us.

As Swarup Singh talks on, the train pulls into Jaipur, the fabled pink city dreamt of by an astronomer king in the seventeenth century. The station, close to the City Palace, is teeming with people, as if the arrival of the train is an excuse for a kind of celebration. The whole platform breaks out into noise and excitement, and even though we have arrived, I am offered all manner of food through the windows – 'for the journey' – as the brakes hiss and the pistons slide to a halt. Tired from too much sitting, we all leave the train. As a porter grabs my bags and hurries off to find a cousin of his who runs a taxi, I take a last look at the other dreamers who accompanied me on this journey. Kailash is off with his friends; O.P. Dixit on his way to his desk. Swarup Singh, still speaking his odd English that is at

Side streets in the 'pink city' of Jaipur

once both the epitome and a caricature of the Queen's English, sets off to meet his former schoolfellows and doubtless to recall the days when Maharajahs ruled on the face of the earth and Jodhpur was as rich as Jaipur. He is hoping for another game of polo in Jaipur, and will dream that he hears the thunder of ponies' hooves, and not just the swish of bicycle tyres.

I will take the waiting taxi to the Rambagh, once a palace, now a hotel, and there I will fall asleep. A train journey is, after all, a pretty exhausting affair, with its strange meetings and exotic tales. The whole of India travelled with me on the Line of Dreams.

ECUADOR
The Good and the Quick
STANLEY REYNOLDS

Quite early in the morning. Before even the sun had got out of bed. On a Graham Greeneish sort of morning full of Latin menace, I hurried along dark streets to mass in Guayaquil. It was the feast day of a nice, respectable English Catholic martyr, the Blessed Thomas Reynolds of Oxford. A bit of a bogus saint, old Blessed Thomas. But one of the family nevertheless. Here in Guayaquil they were celebrating some showy, local saint's day in a gold-encrusted church, with proper beggars already stationed in the beggars' porch: a medieval scene, full of wasted limbs and silent, staring Goya faces. One woman beggar held a baby in her arms. The child did not move. I stopped and looked. The baby was dead. A natty beggar, with a necktie of wild, white dots on scarlet and a flowered shirt, came crawling in on legs amputated at the knees, bumping along, with a smile all gaps and gold teeth, on two knee-pads cut from an old rubber tyre. The tie, I noticed, was the same as mine: the white spots on scarlet silk which the Drones Club had rejected in favour of something in purple.

Strange to think of P.G. Wodehouse here. Or of the Blessed Thomas Reynolds: a quiet English saint, long dead and far removed from the gawdy church full of crippled beggars, old ladies full of wrinkles and Hail Marys and tearful, young whores still up from the night before. I seemed to have gained hours but lost centuries flying from England to Ecuador.

A shoeshine boy came in and prayed before a bank of candles. He wore a picture of Mickey Mouse on his shirt. Above the candles Christ looked down all covered with horrible, open, bleeding wounds. His eyes seemed to have been gouged from their sockets. It seemed a more realistic image of the world to present to a little Ecuadorian shoeshine boy than Mr Walt Disney's cheerful mouse.

I love the lovely little English lines that Sir John Betjeman loves as well: trains clicking through the quiet, secret parts of towns, taking you out to English summer adventures in beer-hazy, rain-washed cricket pavilions, long summer afternoons, all dripping beer tents and greasy sausage rolls; and endless talk of Barlow long ago.

This was something else. Strange and new to me, a traveller only on the 8.24 from Oxford to Paddington. This was something wonderfully romantic. A line which ran from the jungle to the high Andes, linking Guayaquil, called the Pearl of the Pacific, with the capital city of Quito, named The Light of America; only 288 miles but taking a tortuous route: across 309 bridges, through three tunnels, round countless hairpin curves. A little wonder of the world is the Guayaquil–Quito Line.

So I had them pack some sandwiches, some cigars and a bottle of wine at the hotel and headed for the train thinking no more about it than if I were off to Bradford to see Lancashire and Yorkshire play, even smiling that foolish smile I always seem to get when I'm off on a train journey to see a little cricket.

'Gringo,' I heard one of the natives whisper to another one.

Weird fellows they looked, like something out of a movie: straw hats and baggy, white pyjamas, faces like the bandits who try to sell you chocolate on the telly. Then I caught a glimpse of myself in a shop window. I did look like I was out for a day at Hove or Lord's. And a rainy one at that, in my old slouch hat, tweed coat, cardy, Oxford bags and full brogues. The locals stopped and stared. It was as if C. Aubrey Smith had suddenly wandered into town.

The clocktower on Guayaquil waterfront

If you know Joseph Conrad's great book *Nostromo*, well, then you know Guayaquil. Conrad called the city Sulaco in the novel. He called Ecuador Costaguana which is not much of a name but is perhaps better than Ecuador. Even the Ecuadorians don't really like the name. 'Can you imagine,' an old fellow said to me, one of those dignified old Spanish grandee types, with one of those nifty little beards that Shakespeare and Frank Zappa like to wear. 'Can you imagine,' this old fellow said, 'naming a country after a line!'

Well, stepping out of the air-conditioned nightmare of a hotel, one of those modern places that seem to follow you about no matter where you go, you can see that *Nostromo*'s Costaguana hasn't changed very much. It's still the same old, sleazy, steamy, southern coastal town where, I gather, they still do slit a chap's throat for fourpence.

Bright and early in the morning, strolling down the big, wide main street, all full of palm trees and sleeping peons, the old Pearl of the Pacific was looking pretty dusty. Down on the river bank there were a lot of chaps sleeping in the mud. They were fishermen who, in a little while, would be getting up and pushing out up the river in their tiny boats to the open, blue Pacific sea. I still had some time to kill before catching the launch which would take me across the river to the railway station and so I sauntered up the Malecon, this wide and handsome boulevard that faces, in a most civilised and pleasant manner, on the river front, and there I saw the spot where the Spaniards stepped ashore, bringing the Holy Mother Church, whooping cough, measles, the pox (all sorts), civilisation and the common cold. The old town is still there, perched on the side of a hill with, on a clear day such as this, a great, ice-capped volcano looming up far, far away in the distance like some sort of advertisement for air conditioning in all the heat and tropical decay of jungly Guayaquil.

The Spaniard didn't have it all his own way. Drake came here too. He pulled in and raided that little town perched on stilts on the hillside and flayed a Spaniard or two for tea. The Ecuadorians have had a terrible history. And when foreigners weren't sailing in to knock them about they'd have a go at one another. It comes as a surprise to learn they are a cheerful lot, full of jokes and tall stories, the Irish of Latin America.

On the Malecon there is a big statue of the poet Byron and the story about how Byron got to be there tells you a lot about the happy-go-lucky Ecuadorians. The name of the statue doesn't say Byron. It says Almeida, the name of the national poet of Ecuador. The thing was they selected two chaps to get a statue made of Alamada and bundled them off to London to get an artist to make it. Unfortunately the fellows had such a good time in

London they spent all the statue money. It must have been a fearful morning when the two woke up all hungover and realised, counting up the pennies left from the night before, that they had somehow managed to drink away the Ecuadorian national poet. Then one of them had a bright idea and they wandered about the London statue shops and went back home with a nice second-hand Byron. And there Byron stands, standing in for the local boy.

But then I heard a whistle blow and I nodded goodbye to Byron and raced down the gangway to a funny old launch crammed full of local folk and tourists and we chugged across the Rio Guayas, very wide and handsome in the morning light, with just the slightest smell of the salt sea blowing in on the breeze, and with a jolly local engaging me in conversation, telling me about last summer when the ferry turned turtle and all the passengers and crew got ate by the sharks.

'Gosh!' I said.

He didn't seem all that pleased with just a simple gosh.

He turned and tried to tell his story about the sharks to a Japanese tourist sitting alongside us on the bouncing, top-heavy old boat.

'Ha!' the Japanese tourist said.

That didn't please the old man at all.

'*Muchos* hungry *tiburón. Muy Muy* hungry sharks,' the old man said.

'Ha!' the Japanese tourist said. 'Ha! —zzz—Iz zas so?'

The old man looked away in disgust. He spied some German tourists, deep in study of maps and guide books, evidently thought better of it and fell into silent contemplation of the disappointingly finless waves.

Pretty soon the boat bumped into the dock and across a dusty, unpaved, Wild West sort of street stood the dilapidated old railway station of Duran with one of the most cheerful-looking sights you ever will hope to see: a jolly, cheery, cherry-red painted mogul 2–6–0, a splendid old Baldwin from Philadelphia, a working steam loco, standing trembling with steam up, all clanging bells, happy as a sandboy in the shimmering early morning tropical sunshine, jolly as a carnival, a holiday on wheels. And in fact this was fiesta time, August in Latin America on a faraway Oh so romantic Pacific coast, with just the sight of it sending shivers up your arms – thinking, So much for Paddington and the London Underground – with passengers jamming into the first-, second- and third-class carriages, carrying chickens and children and pigs and all manner of fruit, and especially carrying bananas in this, the original Banana Republic of the World, with no less than thirty-seven different kinds of bananas if you cared to count them. Already they were climbing on the top of the train, climbing up onto the roof because there wasn't any more room in third class.

When the sun has sunk down on winter nights in grey London I have sat by the fire and dreamed winter dreams of South American mornings such as this. How far away and long ago seemed all that English drizzle. *Clang clang clang* went the shiny brass bell of the Little Red Engine. Drizzly old England couldn't catch me now.

'Did you remember to pack the flask of tea and the biccies, Brian? I do hope you didn't forget.'

In a bushjacket, round, wire-rimmed specs, a drooping moustache, swept-back hair: an Englishman. Two Englishmen. The other actually wore a cloth cap, cocked down at a jaunty angle, a hooked nose like a young Mr Punch and a pale-red English face, cracked by a smile, and with a set of teeth like a row of condemned houses which spoke of Lancashire.

Clutching a first-class ticket, that cost less than one pound, I squeezed through the rugger scrum of jabbering natives, clucking chickens and squealing pigs to the carriage, painted the same red, called Ecuadorian red, as the locomotive; and while the bell clanged and the hooter hooted I saw that, for all the noise of the station, the town was not yet awake but lay low all around us, quite still, asleep, as the train gave a few more clangs and hoots and moved out through a shanty town.

Wild weeds, tall grass, houses on stilts for the time of floods. Rice fields. Fields of tobacco. Fields of sugar cane. And, of course, bananas. Rice out of the window. Bananas out of the window. Pigs and goats and chickens and ponies and cows and bulls and children and old people and sad faces and faces with smiles all teeth. A lad in a field of sugar cane looked up at me looking down at him from the train window and he laughed to see anything so funny-looking as a gringo like me.

There is breadfruit out of the window. There is wild ginger, with big white flowers smelling of gardenia like the corner florist shop at home in England. There are great mango trees the colour of bright salmon out the window. And a trumpet-shaped blossom hanging drowsily from its branches turns out to be belladonna, sleepy as its name.

How sad and lonely this country looks. Poor and underdeveloped in spite of all the foreigners who came here for gold or to loot and rob it in some other way. The spirit of the belladonna has drifted into the rolling train, and the passengers, who had all been up early, perhaps even as early as me, but for whom perhaps this is only a humdrum, ordinary, everyday sort of trip and not the magic of, at long last, Latin America, but only home to them, fell asleep. Even the beautiful German girl tourists, one blonde and one with red hair, laid their beautiful heads to one side and slept. Their red and golden heads like exotic blooms among all the nodding black-haired heads. Two great, fat Germans, husbands or boyfriends of the sexy sleeping beauties, stuffed to bulging like fat German sausages, sat bolt upright, reading guide books.

Rising to my feet I pushed past the sleeping Indians, the Japanese tourist (wide awake, smiling, inscrutable), and wandered through second class and on to third class, which was nothing but a box car with a narrow, unpadded bench down the middle. I received that special hard look that is reserved for gringos. But how sad they were. Forlorn. And *these*, I thought, were supposed to be *the* happy people of Latin America. The hardness of their lives was apparent in their faces, and the way in which they sat. If one believed, as most of the world's people do believe, in reincarnation, what bad things had these people done in some past life to deserve the lives they lead? Poor Ecuador, with its thirty-seven kinds of bananas.

A newspaper seller came in from first class, looked round and moved on. 'This is that rare thing, *Señor*,' said an Ecuadorian sitting up with me in the hotel bar the night before. He was something big, it seemed, in the tourist trade after it was now, evidently, not such a good thing to be something big in oil. 'Ecuador, *Señor*, is a democracy with a free press.'

Seeing the newspaper seller leave the fourth-class carriage I realised why this was. Of course they could print what they want in the newspapers. Hardly anybody could read.

Back in the first class the blonde-haired German girl and the red-haired German girl were fixing their hair and looking at their pretty faces in little looking-glasses. I wondered what good things they did in a past life to be so lucky in this one now.

'It's not that England doesn't have fast bowlers,' the Lancastrian was saying. 'I'd never say that, would I? We haven't thrown up a pair like Lillee and Thomson since Statham and Trueman. But then the Aussies haven't had anyone like Lillee and Thomson since, well, since Miller and Lindwall.'

I turned to see to whom this intelligence was directed and I was amazed to see it was the Japanese.

'Ha! — zzz — Iz zas so?' the Japanese tourist said.

'Of course they got eight-ball overs over there down under. Same as Lancashire League. Oh aye, we got eight-ball over up in Valley.'

'Ha! — zzz — Iz zas so?' said the Japanese.

'Oh aye,' said the Lancashireman.

'Ryahly, Witherspoon,' said the other Englishman, 'you ryahly are un-controllable. You ryahly ayah.'

Witherspoon, rising to his feet, cap pulled way down over one eye, both hands thrust deep into his pockets, stood jangling his change.

'Well,' he said, 'I think I'll go and make some new friends.'

'Ha! — zzz —' said the Japanese. 'Iz zas so?'

The other Englishman burst out laughing and winked a conspiratorial eye at me.

'Remember, Witherspoon,' he said in standard English, 'we're meeting Pyecroft at Bucay. We can't let old Godders down, now can we? Of course the train will be scandalouslah late. Scandalouslah!'

What an amazing bunch of maniacs the Americans who came to Ecuador to run the railway seem to have been. Likewise the Americans who first built it. The Guayaquil to Quito Line is rare among Latin American railways simply because it was not built by the British, like almost every other line in South America.

Other Latin American countries had been lucky enough to have organisational geniuses happen along and decide to build a railway. There was no Meiggs or Wheelwright or Clark who came to Ecuador. Still, it was badly in need of a railway. Ecuador was one country but it was cut in two, divided by the Andes, which meant it took two weeks to go from the port city of Guayaquil to the mountain capital of Quito.

The line would have to go from sea level to close to 12,000 feet. This was not the highest the Andes could go but the problems were great and it turned out to be the toughest construction job in the Andes because the line had to cross a mountain called the Devil's Nose, the *Nariz del Diablo*.

The Ecuadorian was foolishly optimistic about the business. A rather uncared-for bust of the President of Ecuador at the time, Garcia Moreno, stands among the weeds on the front lawn of the Duran railway station. It was Garcia Moreno, full of the Latin American version of Victorian confidence, who in 1871 got the work started on the line. There was coffee, tobacco and all sorts of fruit in the lowlands and the railway would bring it out to Guayaquil and then up the Pacific coast to California and everybody would grow rich.

Garcia Moreno, who is rather the unsung genius of railway building, used an unusual gauge. Not the normal metre-gauge but a 42-inch narrow track. There is only one other in Latin America, in Chile. This ran through the marshes and rice and sugar country with no trouble at all and then entered the more firm ground where the tropical forest thickens. It was here that the trouble started.

After these first fifty-four miles the track began to rise. Indeed, in the next twenty-seven miles the track would have to go up to 5925 feet at a

Indians sit beside the train at Sibambe

village called Sibambe where the train still stops today. And there, plainly in view, the engineers saw the melodramatic bulk of the Devil's Nose rising high above the railway workers' heads, blocking the line.

There is no gainsaying the tenacity of the Ecuadorians. They were, after all, the inheritors of the Spaniards, and the Conquistadors had come up through the jungle from the sea on the same route as the railway track and the old Spaniards had got themselves and their horses over the Devil's Nose.

For two years the Ecuadorians worked trying to find a way round the Devil's Nose. Then they paused. I suppose they were completely exhausted. They waited for two more years and then, finally, they gave up the ghost. Garcia Moreno himself had also ran out of luck. He suddenly became very unpopular. He was hacked to death one day outside the Presidential palace.

A new hero had come along, however. They never seem to be in short supply in Latin America. This was the colourful General Eloy Alfaro, a fighter, a revolutionary, a man of tremendous energy who was, like Garcia Moreno, also obsessed with the notion of getting a railway completed. The General, in 1897, his first year in office as President, swallowed his Latin pride and decided to ask the gringos. He raised money by selling state bonds in the US and in Britain. Various agreements with several foreign companies were entered into but nothing came of them until Alfaro met Archer Harman, a hard-nosed American businessman with engineering interests. Harman agreed not only to complete the track but also to furnish all the equipment and rolling stock, build the stations along the line, set up the ferry connecting Guayaquil with Duran and then supply the drivers, the brakemen and the conductors to run the railway.

The company was all American, with the single exception of one English-man, a man known by the dandy name of the Honourable St George Lane Fox Pitt. Harman saw his Ecuadorian line rivalling the famous Lima–Oroya in Peru. And making as much money as that fabled line. The Harman line would open trade with the United States through the big port of Guayaquil. In the end, however, nothing worked out as they planned. The twentieth century came and the track was still only sixty miles inland from Guayaquil. That was just six miles in from where the Ecuadorians had left off. In the jungles the Americans died of malaria and snake bite. John Harman, the engineer brother of Archer Harman and a hero of the American Civil War, was killed, along with many others, in a landslide.

They had four locomotives, thirty-five work cars and three thousand labourers but they couldn't get much beyond a place called Bucay. Be-cause the Americans were parked there the town started booming. But the line only crept along. Working full out the Americans managed to lay only twenty-two miles of track by 1901. But that was a tremendous job, they had climbed up through dense forest, gone past innumerable streams and cas-cades. Below them, you can see in old photographs, were the flat lands of the great sugar estates and banana and cocoa plantations and above them, at 5000 feet, stood a line of seemingly impenetrable hills. Bald, colossal rounded hills of granite which even shut out the sunlight.

Some 30,000 coolies had died building just one line in India. The Americans were no more shy about killing labourers than the British were. They could get all the coolies, or peons, they wanted. But throwing 30,000 coolies against these mountains would do no good, especially with the Devil's Nose. What they needed was some sort of trick. The American engineers sat down and worked out a system of inspired switchbacks. They cut a giant Z in the sheer cliff face. A switchback on a gradient of five and a half per cent; four levels of track which finally came to an exhausted halt 8500 feet up. It was one of the most difficult feats of engineering in the entire history of railway construction.

And that was what we were heading for, swaying along through the forest jungle, pulled by the little Baldwin mogul 2–6–0.

The drivers and the brakemen and the ticket collectors are all Ecuadorians now. They took over the running of the railway for themselves during the Second World War. But before that there were these amazing roughnecks, the wild-eyed gringos from America and Britain who ran it for them and whose colourful story has not really been told to date. In Duran there are still some people who remember the American railway workers, known as boomers. There it was I picked up the words of a song the boomers used to sing. To the tune of 'Clementine' it went:

Oh Collectors, oh Inspectors, hear the travelling public roar,
And when we are gone forever, they'll forget us nevermore!
Oh the happy days we passed there,
Oh numbers one, two, three and four,
Chuckin' drunks and checkin' chickens
On the trains in Ecuador.

The idea of being remembered – 'they'll forget us nevermore' – seems to have been a false hope. Five years ago the unsentimental Ecuadorians wanted to build a football pitch on the site of the American graveyard along the side of the tracks. They brought in a bulldozer and simply cleared the field. Well, I don't suppose those early Americans were sentimental types either. I found a list of their names, the names of the pioneer drivers and brakemen. They are like something out of a cowboy movie. Smilie MacIntosh, Lucky Baldwin, Nigger MacRae, Kid Dalton, Cat Jamieson, Bull Wilson, Hurricane Harry and Roaring Dick.

The boomers all carried single-action ·44 Frontier Colts. There is a story about a young Scotsman, John L. Macintyre, who left the peace and quiet of the Caledonian Railway to come to Latin America, and brought with him for protection a small Webley ·32. 'Say, sonny,' an old-timer said to him, 'if you was to shoot that off at me and I got to know about it, I'd be real mad at you.' Scotty Macintyre went out and bought himself a big Colt ·44. 'I couldn't believe my eyes,' he said, 'when I first saw men pull guns on each other.'

That was in 1910. The American West was tamed by then. The wilder spirits were forced to come to Latin America. A freight conductor named Felton was famous among the boomers for his fast draw. He was able to walk down a street drawing and shooting and keeping a tin can in the air all the time.

'The first time I ever saw him was in Ambato,' Scotty Macintyre told a visiting American reporter in the 1950s, 'in 1910 and he was walking down the street with a gun in each hand, keeping a tin can on the move ahead of him with *unaimed* shots from his six-shooters.'

The recollections of the pioneer railway men are filled with the most appalling sort of prejudice against the local natives. There was a rather amusing, but ghastly, fellow who had spent a lifetime in Ecuador and still could speak no Spanish. Any time an Ecuadorian would address him in Spanish he'd simply say, 'Me Gringo – me no savvy.'

'You know, Scotty,' this man said to Macintyre one day, 'I don't savvy this lingo at all. Why in hell they want to say *"naranja"* instead of "orange" beats me. But you are an educated hombre, Scotty, speakin' three lingos like you do – Scotch, English an' American!'

Nice old-fashioned violence those stories of the early railway boomers are, all safely in the past. It makes you feel nostalgic for the good old, bad old days when there were frontiers to conquer, when a man could go out and win the West and never ever even had to change his shirt. What with education and the price of whisky, you think, those days are gone forever, but it is not so. There are towns in Ecuador today just as wild as Duran in the early years of this century. These are the oil towns and they are full of pistol-packing oilmen from all over the United States and Europe. But the railway doesn't run there and so they were no concern of mine.

With the sun right up new in a clear blue, powder blue, cloudless sky it was a splendid sight, leaning out of the window watching the little red engine weaving its way through all the bright green of the forest jungle, with the red and the blue and the green looking cozy as an illustration in a children's book. I looked at my watch and it was still not opening time in England. I left the drink where it was in the shade of my canvas bag.

We passed through a town called Yaguachi where a fiesta was about to start. Fantastic trains were already pulling into town. They seemed to have got hold of every bit of rolling-stock available to bring the crowds to Yaguachi that morning. They were leaning out of the doors and windows, there was standing room only on the tops of the trains and flat cars had been pressed into service to carry the faithful to town to celebrate yet another little local saint who, I am sure, no Pope in Rome has ever recognised. An Indian in a felt hat and one of those handwoven capes, which are very trendy and cost a fortune in the King's Road, explained to me that there had been a terrible epidemic in 1927. An epidemic of what I could not quite grasp. But it was something awful anyway. Everyone was ill with it. Many died. Then a miracle happened. Every year since then they have poured into the little town where they worship at the church there, a church which was once a little church but is now a vast place, he said, to hold the annual crowd. A battery of priests give out Holy Communion all day long. Then, at nightfall, the weary priests go home to bed and the music and the dancing and the drinking start.

I started scribbling all this down in my notebook when I suddenly felt eyes upon me. Looking up I saw them all gaping at me. Children, and grown-ups too. And that was the way it continued all through the journey. Every time I took a pen to paper a crowd of Indians collected to gape and wonder for they cannot read or write and the sight of someone scribbling

Steam locomotive and train running down the main street in Milagro

swiftly across a blank page is a sight to wonder at. Outside there would be amazing things to see, sheer drops of a thousand feet, hair-raising hairpin curves, majestic, ice-capped volcanoes glowing in the air across a great expanse of desert. But none of these was such a wondrous sight as seeing the gringo scribble.

Wonder, in fact, was the grand name of the next little town: Milagro, a town called Miracle; a place of yet another fantastic happening not really all that long ago. Once, you think, our own ancestors lived like that in Britain and Europe when miracles were certainly very miraculous things, a certain source of wonder, but not all that rare when you really get down to adding them all up. We've lost all that. And the poor, cold-blooded Yankees in North America have never had any miracles although the Devil was, at one time, always at work in such places as Salem up in cold and rocky Protestant Massachusetts. In South America the Devil didn't get such a look in and miracles are, apparently, still happening.

Why only just as recently as 1957 on this very line, my Indian informant told me, this very train caught on fire going through a particularly tricky bit of mountain pass. The brakeman, who was on the roof of the train, knelt down and prayed to the Virgin; and she blew the fire out or, at least, caused a sudden downpour which put it out. If I didn't believe him, well, he said, I only had to go to the little church in the mountains, just outside Riobamba, and there I would see for myself a painting, done very properly in oil colours, on one wall of the church, showing the train all ablaze, with the brakeman kneeling in prayer and the Blessed Virgin, very splendidly represented, gorgeous as a jungle bird, looking down on the pious brakeman.

But then, of course, my Indian fellow traveller said, he really should apologise for he could see, and he hoped I would not be too insulted, that I was a gringo and therefore a Protestant or possibly something even worse. Not a bit of it, I told him, I was indeed a Catholic. This was very amazing, he said. On one single morning he had seen not only a gringo writing with wondrous rapidity but also a gringo who was a Catholic. And they were one and the same. He had heard tell of gringo Catholics, most particularly of the late John Kennedy, whose ancestors had come from some island near England where everyone had red hair and all the men wore skirts. Did I come from that island and wear a skirt when I was at home? No, I said, I did not come from that island myself although I had been there and seen the red hair and all the men in skirts and to another place near England where the men wore even more skirts and that was a fine place as well.

The world was a wonderful place, he said. In his village they had set up a television set on the wall of the shop at the crossroads and everyone had seen the wedding of the Prince of England and the golden-haired princess. He knew it was real, he said, but a lot of the silly people in his village thought it was all just a dream.

Did I know the Prince of England? Oh yes, I said, we belonged to the same club, it was called the Punch Table and once you had carved your initials in the wood of the table, why then you were a member and could eat there every week for so long as you lived and never pay anything at all for the food. Some red-haired men from the island of the skirts came to eat there but wore trousers when they did.

Life was truly incredible, he said. The more he lived, he said, the more he wondered at it.

I heard one of those loud, baying, *Haw haw haw* sort of laughs, like the disgusting barristers at El Vino in Fleet Street go in for, and looked up and saw the Englishman looking at me. He obviously spoke Spanish. So I told my Indian pal all about the Blessed Thomas Reynolds, and Saint Richard Reynolds, too, and how they probably, in their own time, went about putting fires out, although there were no strict records of it, and how they were such saintly fellows that the Protestant gringos couldn't stand it any more so they took them out and hanged and drew and quartered them.

Locomotive cab and crew on the line near Naranjito

Together? my Indian asked.

No, I said, one at a time and with some long passage of years in between. It was, however, no longer the practice, I assured him, and I was myself living in relative safety.

We stopped at Naranjito, a town named after orange trees with the trees and the oranges looking like golden lamps in a green night, as in Marvell's poem. A group of beautiful, black-haired schoolgirls, in prim and dazzling white dresses, suddenly appeared on the dusty road in the dappled shade of the tall, green palm trees. They were girls from some upper strata of the tiny village life, with more than a touch of the Spaniard in their long limbs and elegantly placed heads. One even had blue Spanish eyes, behind her long, dark lashes, set at a sexy angle above high, curved, Indian cheekbones. A great beauty and perhaps a little aware of it as she walked across the little wooden bridge that arched the bright, flowing Chan Chan river and mounted the train and entered the first-class carriage, with all the other convent schoolgirls in their white frocks smelling of fresh ironing.

Along about now I thought I'd have a go at something I always wanted to do. So, as the train started pulling out, I brushed past the Japanese tourist, the Englishman, the Teutonic beauties and the Ecuadorian white-frocked roses, jumped down from the train and raced to the engine to ride the footplate. They'd hardly throw me off, what with the train going full speed and me a gringo wearing a collar and practically a Drones Club tie.

I clambered onto the swaying, greasy engine on my hands and knees. A pudgy, red-haired hand helped me to my feet. 'Have a drop of this,' said Witherspoon, holding out a bottle with a Scottish whisky label. 'This is José,' he said, indicating a smiling engine driver, 'and this is young, I dunno, his mate.' 'José's forty-two,' Witherspoon said. 'He lives in Cajabamba, up the line, with his wife and three kids, two sons and a daughter, although, like a lot of the railwaymen, he's got another wife and three kids, all sons, further up the line somewhere. It's macho, see. *Muy hombre* like to have a couple of wives and lots of kiddiewinks. I haven't found out how many families Young What's His Name has, not yet at least I haven't.'

Underneath my feet the footplate was dancing, doing a wild Ecuadorian rumba.

'Go ahead,' said Witherspoon, smiling that smile which was like Salford in the good old days, 'have a belt.'

I took a slug from the bottle marked scotch; after all, somewhere in England early morning topers must already be standing about the pub doors contemplating their watches. Any time, at the best of times, this would have tasted like paraffin, perhaps even turpentine.

Witherspoon and his two new friends, José and Young Thingy, bent double in the rocking cab and slapped and punched each other to control their laughter. The pit of my stomach burned. My lips were on fire. 'It's some native hootch,' Witherspoon said. 'I think it makes you go blind.' He turned to Young What's His Name and asked in Spanish: 'Does this make you go blind? Or does it only make your hair fall out?'

'No, no,' said Young Thingy. He put his forearm between his legs and brought it up, making a fist.

'Sophisticates,' Witherspoon said to me in English. 'Monkey,' he said in Spanish to the young Ecuadorian loco man, 'they'll be putting you in a cage soon and charging people to look at you.' Witherspoon spoke Spanish with a most amazing Lancashire accent but the driver and his young mate thought he was the soul of wit.

There was a sort of thumping behind us on the footplate and turning we saw the other Englishman, climbing up over the roof of the train. Once on top he got to his feet and walked as nonchalantly as you please on the swaying roof, saying, 'Excuse me, please' and 'If you don't mind' and even 'Excuse I' to the thunderstruck Indians under foot, all the time absolutely beaming at us, like Bertram Wooster himself taking a stroll down Bond Street in a brand new pair of purple spats.

'Wot ho Witherspoon!' he said, bouncing down on the footplate with no more thought to the danger than if he were stepping off the kerb. 'I thought your Japanese was the absolute limit,' he said to Witherspoon. 'I mean, he was right out of William Gerhardie's *The Polyglots*. I think, actually, Brian, he might have been having you on with that *Ha! zzz* and *Iz zas so?* but, Witherspoon, you telling him about the Lancashire League's eight-ball overs was as nothing compared to our friend here explaining about the Punch Table to some Indian back there. I didn't quite catch how Prince Charles, Lady Di and your ancestors, the saints, figured into all that, but it was ryahly disgraceful, scandalous and mighty rum. Good morning, chaps,' he said to José and Young What's His Name.

There are some Englishmen, appalling grammar-school swots or from dreadful, minor public schools, who go up to Oxford or Cambridge and never quite get over it but remain undergraduates all their lives. It's a most pleasant way to be and highly recommended if you've got enough money and are, as Bertram might say, oofy enough to be cushioned against the old slings and arrows. This was one of them.

'Pickerstaff,' he said. I thought for a moment he was talking about some obscure piece of Victorian ironmongery which was a vital part of the mogul 2–6–0. But no. It was his name. The bilingual Witherspoon was the local man for some big firm back home in England and Pickerstaff was the man from head office on a flying visit.

'A right prat is Pickerstaff, the git,' Witherspoon confided to me much later on.

Witherspoon was one of those Englishmen who are as much a part of the Latin American scenery as the Amazon or the Andes. He had drifted into Ecuador more than ten years before, stopping in Quito simply because that was where his money ran out, working as a barman and then buying his own pub, selling that and entering half a dozen moderately successful business ventures in as many years, the local rep of several firms back home in England, married to a white-skinned Ecuadorian beauty of very definite Spanish stock: the product of a mean, backstreet, Salford slum, wedded to an heiress of the original Conquistadors: she bearing him fat, red-haired children, and he elevated socially beyond all dreams he may perhaps have had in the rain-wet back alleys of Manchester in the grim late 1940s when he was preparing to fail his eleven-plus and then pick up a taste for foreign climes fighting the King's enemies in Korea and the Queen's in Malaya and at Suez until he had served his time and then set out to see still more of the wide world. Drake's men must have been like him. There are a lot of them in Ecuador like Witherspoon.

And Pickerstaff too, now, also had the air of the Empire builder about him. Watching him sauntering about, absolutely strolling, hands in pockets, across the top of the train, taking the morning air: you could see that this was the sort of idiot that painted the maps red. 'Yorkshire,' Witherspoon sneered. He meant Pickerstaff was showing off. It was a Lancashire sort of an insult. 'An' when they're not showin' off,' said Witherspoon, 'they're bowin' 'n scrapin' like. Oh, aye, Geoffrey Boycott cringin' before Yorkshire committee. Brian Close and even Shillin'worth goin' back to Yorkshire cap in hand. Very Yorkshire that.'

I thought of the Red Rose braving the breeze over Old Trafford and I nodded in grave agreement.

Still, Pickerstaff was a daring fellow; and he wasn't all that drunk, not really.

'Look at them Indians up there,' said Witherspoon. 'Just sittin' there all glum. I saw a bunch of them up in the mountains once, just settin' on th' floor like, all glum like that, an' then suddenly they all burst out wi' laughin'. "Ah wonder what they're laughin' at?" Ah asked a fellow wi' me standin' there, he were a Yank. "Probably," he said, "somethin' Pizarro said."'

On we went to a town called Barraganetal, which was a rare sort of place, with no local saint, but with all the town turned out to see the train come in, right smack down the centre of the High Street: all clanging bells and the whistle blowing off little puffs of white cloud and everybody smiling like mad because this was the big moment of the morning when the train came in, bringing all sorts of strange things from Guayaquil down on the coast: fish from the sea – some sort of local herring – and fruit and sugar cane and newspapers, for those who can read, and relatives for a visit and exotic gringo tourists from so far far away that no one can really believe it, from strange, outlandish places where the men all wear skirts or where a woman rules: lands where everybody can read and write, but in a language such as you never heard the like before; from some places even where they are able to write with such skill that they all write backwards and read turning the pages from back to front. All of this the train brings in the morning. If it wasn't for the train there would be no fish from the sea and no strangers who come from the world that we, *señor*, only see on the television screen or travel all the way up the line to Riobamba to see in the cinema.

It is like that all up the line. Everywhere the train runs right down the middle of the main street and everyone smiles at it and waves at it and makes the most marvellous thing of it. They have not come rushing out of their houses to see an ancient steam locomotive, the way we tourists have travelled six thousand miles to see it. No, the steam engine is quite normal

Consolidation 45 runs up the main street in Alausi while diesel 161 waits on the right

to them, but the train is a moving market-place from which you buy things or sell things to. Plus, it is large and noisy and colourful. A bit of life.

The Chan Chan is a bright, swiftly flowing river that runs along the line of the track. Everywhere you see the Indian women doing their washing in it. The clothes are bright, dashing reds and blues and yellows. The women kneel at the river bank, pounding the clothes on rocks. A scene from another time. The Chan Chan flashes on, heading towards the sea and we are running upstream against it, crossing and recrossing it on these colourful old rickety-rackety bridges, sometimes perched at a precarious angle which makes you stop and wonder if they really do make sure that these old tracks and all the old, rotting timber are all that safe.

In Bucay we change the locomotive. The nice little toytown red mogul is a beautiful sight to be sure but it has not the puff for the high Andes. You couldn't get over the Devil's Nose or race across the terrifying Alausi loops in the little red engine. For the high Andes they pull out of the battered, run-down sheds at Bucay this glorious, big, black-painted Baldwin Consolidation 2–8–0. A great brute of a steam engine especially rigged out for the tortuous pull ahead.

Climbing down from the engine Witherspoon decided he'd have a shoe-shine. It was, he said, a habit he had picked up in all his years in Ecuador. The shoeshine boys come down from some little mountain village to ply their trade in Bucay. They are from a family of innumerable children and no father. This is no rare thing but it strikes you as odd in so Catholic a country. Why should these fathers suddenly pull up stakes one day and go off, not, apparently, to seek the freedom of the single life, but to find some other woman and raise even more shoeshine boys. All of Latin America is full of these poor children, hundreds of thousands of them abandoned by their families, pushed out into the streets of all the big cities. You wonder what the Pope could be thinking when he praises family life to these poor people.

The shoeshine boys here are lucky, country lads who at least still have a mother. Barefoot and dirty they ride the top of the train down to Bucay where they sleep under the stars on the bare, wooden boards of the station's front porch. Caesar, my shoeshine boy, is twelve and his little pal is eleven and so shy in front of me that he could not properly speak his name. The same age as my own sons back safe in England where they are at a Catholic public school and pull faces because they have to shine their own shoes.

Caesar and his pal cannot read or write. They are not brothers but pals, and pals in the cutthroat world of shining shoes. When they have finished they stand with their arms round each other and are so brave and good that you think, well, something must be all right here which produces such fortitude and affection. Caesar and his little pal are dirty and they stink, but they shine like a good deed in a naughty world.

They were changing their locos in the middle of the main street when the dreadful Pickerstaff suddenly cried out: 'There he is, there's Pyecroft, old Godders, riding on the footplate.' A tall, middle-aged Englishman in a white shirt, rolled up to the elbows, beamed down from the big Consolidation cab. Then skipped down and shook hands all round, grasping my hand as well.

'I've got something for you,' he announced. He guided us into the sudden, cool shade of the railway sheds. 'There!' he said.

'Oh yes?' said Pickerstaff.

'Oh aye?' said Witherspoon.

People settle themselves on the roof of the train while a pig roots for food in
Bucay High Street

'Yes, indeed,' said Pyecroft, old Godders.

This was, in fact, a rare sight for the railway buff. Several old Manchester-built Garratts standing there, in various states of decomposition. They're not in service. They keep cannibalising these engines, to keep the others rolling. And soon, of course, there won't be anything left. Then, no more steam.

Old Godders was the true railway buff; compared to him the rest of us were mere fakers. He ran some sort of business on the coast in which he was tremendously successful. But he lived for railways.

'I've been on the footplate of every loco in Ecuador,' he said. 'They all know me. I never have to pay. I just come along, and hop on for a little ride.'

And all the rest of Latin America lay open to him. For him Latin America was not a place of cruel dictatorships, beautiful women, exotic jungles, high mountains, big rivers, strange food and an incomprehensible history. It was a vast railway museum.

Pickerstaff thought he was a great bore. But, like all men who really know about something, the eccentric Pyecroft, who was the sort of man you might see any day in the West End of London, stepping out of the back of a Rolls-Royce or Bentley, distinguished, in a very good suit from Savile Row and excellent shirting from Jermyn Street, could never be boring when he spoke about railways. I could not reproduce here words that would give anything but the smallest tip of the iceberg of his great knowledge. He knew it all, back to front and front to back, and then sideways, and he had such enthusiasm, and such jolly, sparkling eyes when he talked about his subject, that even if you did not know a word that he was saying, you would still be intrigued by all the pleasure it obviously gave him to talk about it.

'Old Godders does go on a bit,' Pickerstaff said. 'It's like Lord Emsworth going on about his pig.' The ghastly Pickerstaff had no notion of what a bore he was himself. He only seemed to come to life and give a little pleasure when he was showing off, walking along the top of the train. For the rest of it his repertoire was undergraduate stuff, talking in funny voices and pulling faces. You got the idea that he hadn't made up these routines for himself but was copying it off someone he had once known who had done it properly.

But that is the way with train journeys. You get stuck with people. And, of course, it is the people you meet on the trains who often count more than the trip. Pickerstaff, after all, was some sort of a buff. He could have been back in Guayaquil getting drunk and making a slob of himself. Perhaps that was his true nature. He had, however, somehow surmounted that and had struck out for adventure. You had to give him that.

'I can only go with you to Huigra,' Godfrey Pyecroft said. 'Then I must be back in Guayaquil. It's business.' He spoke with that weird, high voice English speakers get when they have lived too long among Spanish speaking peoples. It was a squeaky, mouse-like voice. Pickerstaff quickly mastered the hang of it and spoke very little else until he really got drunk and fell into the 'ryahly disgraceful' and 'absolutely scandalous' voice of Sidney Quarles or one of Aldous Huxley's other comic, upper-class Englishmen of the early novels.

The train started giving very serious hoots and finally the passengers took some notice of it and climbed back on board. The train took on a transformation now. Because we would be doing some serious climbing from now on they had not only switched locos but also taken a number of carriages off the train. So there we all were, all three classes, first, second and third, crammed in together in four coaches; and, naturally, up on the roof as well.

The gregarious Witherspoon, rough-hewed northcountryman that he was, had made some more new friends in the carriage: a young American girl and her aunt, whom she was visiting in Ecuador. The Ecuadorian auntie was a lesson in political science. She was a trim, forty-fiveish woman, with fading blonde hair done up like Eva Perón used to do hers, wearing a neat light-blue suit, which, I suppose, she thought matched her eyes. Metaphysically she wore white gloves and spoke in very careful English. The American niece, her sister's girl, was fifteen, blonde of hair and blue of eye, with about six thousand dollars' worth of braces on her teeth. It was a great misfortune to befall a teenage blonde but she seemed, in the way of American children and dentistry, to take it well. She knew, you reckoned, that in a year or two she would be a great heartbreaker with a dazzling, wrap-around smile of white teeth.

The American niece clutched some fifteen hundred dollars' worth of camera to her bosom and gazed about, eager for something to snap. She announced rather solemnly: 'I'm going to take a picture.' Except she was so American she made a question of it. Because of this it sounded most odd. The earnest, almost threatening declaration ended with a note of doubt. 'I'm going to take a picture?'

We looked about us for her subject. 'I just gotta take a picture of those Indians?'

'Not dey Hindians,' the Ecuadorian auntie said. 'Why do always the Americans and foreigners have to take pictures of dey Hindians. I wish dey go away.'

'Who,' I asked, 'the Americans and the foreigners?'

'No,' said the Ecuadorian auntie, 'dey Hindians. Everyone wants them to go away but dey will not go away.'

'Oh, I just gotta take a picture of this?' the American niece said, looking at some more Indians.

'The Hindians dey are so sad,' the Ecuadorian auntie said. 'Dey music is very sad.'

As if on cue someone put a transistor radio on and it played a sad, Indian song from the mountains of Ecuador.

'Des is a sad Indian song from Ecuador,' said the auntie. 'It is a song that says dat after life what will be left?'

'And what does it say will come after life?'

'No, no,' said the auntie. 'Not dey after life like dat. What do dey Hindians know of soul? Dey Hindians do not care about dey soul. No, in this sad song of the Hindians they wonder what will the earth be like when they are dead. That is all.'

'And how will the earth be after they are dead?'

'Why,' the Ecuadorian auntie said, 'just the same as always. Dey will be sunshine. Dey will be moonshine also.'

The song, she said, was called *Vasija de Barro* which sounded pretty romantic but in English meant Mask of Mud which isn't very romantic at all.

The Ecuadorian auntie was a curious case. She obviously had a great feeling for the haunting music of the Indians of the Andes. She loved the

Consolidation 53 waits outside Huigra station

music, responded to it, but did not like at all the Indians who produced it.

'Do not take any more photographs of dey Hindians, please,' she asked her niece. Who did, indeed, seem to be overdoing it. Still, the Indians have such extraordinary faces. Beautiful, like something made of some special, highly polished wood. 'Why does she want to take pictures of Hindians? When I go to New York dey say to me, de people, "Why you are from Ecuador, how come you are not Hindian?" Why do dey think all Ecuadorians are Hindians? We do not want de Hindians.'

Outside the Indians started appearing in earnest now. Lovely, romantic figures climbing the hills with great loads upon their backs. There is an old Ecuadorian joke about people sitting round watching an Indian carrying some awesome burden up a mountainside and deciding that something must be done for the Indians. Someone suggests getting him a cart, but the wheels would be no good in the mountains. Others suggest other things. Then someone, at last, suggests the obvious: 'Why not get him another Indian?'

Anyway, it was getting long past luncheon and the train was running dreadfully late. The train is always late. But then, who ever came to Latin America just to be on time?

When the Americans built the railway they established the American system of feeding the passengers. It has long since disappeared from the railways of America. Ecuador may be the last country where the old-fashioned American system is used. There is no mystery about it. What happens is

Roast pig is consumed beside the train

that when the train arrives for lunch they bring it onto the train. But what scenes this creates at Huigra, the lunchtime stop, with long chorus lines of felt-hatted Indian women singing out about the contents of their steaming bowls of chicken soup, their great platters of hot corn on the cob, poor little hamsters roasted on wooden sticks, whole little pigs, great pieces of roast pork, and even a whole head of a pig. And, of course, great plates of oranges, pineapples, melons, and fruit for which there seemed to be no English name, and bananas fresh and whole or done in a dozen different ways. They stand and sell this by the side of the train, they bring it onto the train, pass it through the opened windows and stretch up to hand it to the chaps on the roof; and it is all served on proper crockery, no paper plates and plastic cups. The munching and the gnashing of teeth, however, is something frantic, enough to put you off the dainty sandwiches packed long ago in the dark kitchen of the hotel in Guayaquil.

And after they have fed the five thousand the greatest sight of all is the clamour, as the train is starting, to see them trying to pass back the empty plates, shoving them back through the windows, with the servant girls racing alongside the moving train, or expertly handing them down from the roof top. Some giggling young waitresses got caught on the train. They did not seem to mind. When the train slowed, crossing once again the now roaring Chan Chan, falling down from some great height in the mysterious Andes above our heads, the waitresses skipped off the train with their plates all depleted and started walking slowly back to Huigra at a leisurely pace, all very happy and smiling in the sun.

What fish that river should produce. I kept thinking of Negley Farson's great story about fishing in the Andes, one of the best fishing stories ever written. But here I never saw a fisherman, not once all the way along that long stretch of beautiful water just made by God for trout. Farson had fished in Chile. There the rivers had been stocked by an Englishman. Here, too, an angling Englishman had come and stocked the river with trout. But the Indians had dynamited them out, greedy for large catches. They took all the trout. It made you feel some sympathy for the Ecuadorian aunties who wished all the Indians would simply go away. But then the art of the fly and rod are toys for highly civilised, leisured men.

Jack London wrote a story about an Indian dynamiting fish; and John Steinbeck, in *Cannery Row* and *Tortilla Flat*, wrote with similar sympathy of the Mexicans. In Ecuador there is only one writer who writes with such sympathy about the Indians. This is Jorge Icaza, the author of *Huasipungo*. The other Ecuadorian novelists are too busy, it seems, trying to write the Great Spanish American Novel. They are no doubt read by the Ecuadorian auntie who would like to identify with European subtlety. You cannot blame her, and the innumerable Ecuadorians like her, for wanting to identify with Europe. She was, she told me, German on her mother's side. Her grandfather came from Danzig, when it was the German city of Thomas and Heinrich Mann. The German connection explained her blonde hair, blue eyes, and curious accent.

'He knew nothing of Ecuador except dat it was on dey equator so he came dressed in shorts and dey pith helmet and damned near died of dey cold,' she said.

The Indians, naturally, have no connection with Europe. Except one. Their religion. Brought by the old Spaniards and forced upon them with fire and sword.

All the time I travelled out that early morning I kept thinking of the first Spaniards who had come to Ecuador. The great hidalgo, Pedro de Alvarado, Cortez's number one in Mexico, had landed on the beach at Duran with many Spaniards and thousands of Indian bearers from the jungles of Guatemala where he was governor. They had come through the same jungle as us. In the heat of the jungle their armour rusted. They were used to that. They were the tough conquerors of Mexico. Renaissance men, men of the great rebirth, full of themselves in a way that we will never be. Pizarro, a great thug, had taken what we know as Peru from the Incas. The Incas, however, were still in possession of Ecuador. Quito was the summer capital of the Incas, protected by a great army. Alvarado was going to march to it and steal the Inca gold; plus convert the pagans to Christ.

Another, much smaller, band of Spaniards, some two hundred men under Benalcazar, was marching on Quito on a more pleasant route, riding along the Royal Road of the Incas, one thousand miles from deep in Peru to Quito in the far north. Alvarado thought he'd get there first, using the short cut, through the jungle and up the mountains.

And before me now I saw the great canyon of the Chan Chan river which he had faced, with the vast bulk of the *Nariz del Diablo*, the Devil's Nose, blocking out the sunlight, casting us in shadow as we snaked up to it. Leaning out of the window, or out over the edge of the platform, you can see the train disappearing round great bends and then appear again going the other way. While all the time, down below, looking straight down it dropped away to nothing. A thousand feet, a sheer drop down to tiny houses and miniaturised cattle grazing on the green pasture below.

I broke out a bottle of Chilean wine, called *Diablo*, which I brought along to toast the Devil's Nose. Pickerstaff, naturally, drank it all, hot as it was from the heat of the jungle. A grand sight Pickerstaff was, seated on the platform, legs dangling over the edge of the world, drinking wine as if he were seated back home in his own dreadful back garden.

The Chan Chan river wound somewhere away from us as we headed straight on for the Devil's Nose. The mountain, a big, bald piece of granite like a giant, hooked pirate's nose stood before us, blocking our path. A sharp looking brakeman – smoked spectacles, cool-looking shades like someone in a Jack Kerouac novel, a rolled newspaper thrust into his back pocket – glided effortlessly down from the roof and did something deft with the big brake wheel.

It was a terrifying setting. The drop straight down. The rusting track. The rotten wooden ties. A reassuring sight was the cool brakeman. But then that ass Pickerstaff had to start distracting the brakeman with asinine questions.

'I say, are the carriages always painted the same colour?'

'No,' the cool brakeman said.

'Why not?' Pickerstaff, the absolute idiot, asked.

'It all depends,' said the cool brakeman, signalling to another brakeman down the train.

Below was the great, green wall of the Andes, sometimes covered in cloud and then breaking through, a spectacular green. Ahead I caught sight of the engine erupting like a volcano, all black smoke, and could hear the eight spinning drivers of the 2–8–0 slipping and then gripping, and I could see it leaning into a tight corner, with the whole length of the train

View from the train as it climbs the Devil's Nose

tipped to one side, with me wondering what was keeping us from toppling over, with the whole train drifting down to earth and destruction far below where the cows in the fields were only dots.

It was then I saw the Dare Devil Riders of the Devil's Nose: a pack of wild teenagers, who came running alongside the track and then hopped on to the side of the train, holding on with one hand and leaning far out over absolutely nothing at all for a thousand feet. All of them laughing and having a grand time trying to knock each other off.

On the Devil's Nose we started racing backwards on the first of the switchbacks, the zigzag, that carry you up the mountain face. This is no ordinary train ride. It is like something out of the funfair, only writ large. I knew if anyone was watching me they would see that my face had gone white. I felt somebody press up to me. It was the American niece. 'That's nice?' she said, and snapped away at this extraordinary scenery all round us.

Well, we had come up the Devil's Nose and I was feeling mighty proud of myself for not fainting dead away. Then they hit me with the Alausi Loop. Once you have come up the Devil's Nose you think you have surmounted the great dangerous thing. All the guide books talk of nothing but the Devil's Nose. For some reason they never mention the Alausi Loop: the three hairpin curves. It is a fantastic thing. At one point it runs round the lip of a volcano. The soil here is volcanic, sandy stuff, and each day it erodes by anything up to six centimetres. A railway crew is kept at work

Consolidation 53 follows the switchback up the Devil's Nose

all day, every day, geeing up the track, fighting against this continuous erosion. Since the line opened the track has given way some five hundred metres. None of that seemed very safe to me.

Going through the Alausi Loop is like a dream of flying. The high altitude is probably what makes it seem unreal and dreamlike. All around me passengers had dropped off to sleep. The beautiful German girls were dozing while out the window was everything they had come all those miles and paid all that money to see.

'You have turned quite dey different colour,' the Ecuadorian auntie said to me. 'You know,' she said, 'I took an American woman from California, a cousin, on this journey and she said to me, "I see dat in Ecuador you do not need drugs." '

Most of the tourists were not asleep but were leaning out of the window, taking pictures or merely looking open-mouthed at all the splendour; and into the middle of all this excitement came an Indian woman, shouting out the name of something she was trying to sell. She stood there shouting out this incomprehensible name of something to eat and then shook her head in disgust at all these foreigners who wanted merely to gaze stupidly out the windows when they could be eating this good thing she had to sell.

Was there ever a train journey like this? One in which the scenery changes so suddenly over such a short distance? At a tiny place called Palmira we, who had thought all the time that we had been up about as

The top of the Devil's Nose is finally reached by Consolidation 53

high as we would ever go, started to see that here we were really climbing: high into the high Andes, with the most amazing scenery outside the window as the train crept along through the long, cloudless afternoon and into the evening.

The great Pedro de Alvarado had finally managed to get his men out of the jungle and over the mountains right here. All of his horses had died in the attempt, and eighty-six Spaniards also. Now, horseless out of the mountains, he met a vast inhospitable desert, icy cold at night, and with the prospect of more mountains before him on the far horizon. The snowy cold of the mountains had killed off most of his Indian bearers who were from the steamy lowlands of Guatemala. Alvarado – handsome as a hero out of some 1930s Hollywood movie, handsome and dashing as Errol Flynn – who was so dazzlingly good-looking that the Mexicans thought he must be related to the sun itself, was the great hero of Cortez's conquest of New Spain. There is a spot in modern Mexico City which is called Alvarado's Leap, marking the place where the brave Conquistador had made this incredible jump while cutting his way through the fierce Aztec army of Montezuma.

But here on the icy desert he saw something that took the heart right out of him. What he saw was not the Inca army waiting for him. He would not have flagged at such a thing. What defeated him was the sight of horses' hoof prints in the sand. He realised that Benalcazar, with 200 mounted

Spaniards, had beaten him to the punch. Coming along the Royal Road they were already far ahead of Alvarado, heading for Quito, the Light of America, city of Inca gold.

He abandoned his march. Turned back to Guayaquil. Stepped out of history.

And now what a sight was before us! Even Pickerstaff and Witherspoon were struck dumb with awe; and old Godders, the railway buff, poet of Latin American rolling stock, who had decided he would keep on with us despite the call of business on the coast, forgot the nineteenth-century ironmongery long enough to marvel at the prospect before us.

It was the volcanoes. There they stood, looming up, glowing peaks of ice, out there where the flat, eerie desert ended on the horizon. A whole litany of volcanoes. Cotopaxi. The Grand Cayambe. Fiery Sanjay. The Majestic Antisana. Iliniza. A beautiful volcano called The Altar. Corazon. And the Venerable Chimborazo. A landscape as old as the world. It was odd to think that the Incas worshipped the sun when they had these mountains to kneel before.

Now the mountains have a prosaic use. Sixteen thousand feet up on the snowline of Chimborazo there was, I knew, a fellow chipping away great blocks of ice, to bring down to Riobamba, which was the big city in these parts, so the folk could have cold drinks and ice-cream.

Night fell upon us crossing the desert, with the fading sun causing the old steam engine to cast a giant shadow on the sand, and this was very beautiful to watch. Some mountain mist came down at the tale end of the evening: it looked as if we were suddenly travelling through snow, like a scene from *Anna Karenina*. I felt pretty good now about my tweed coat, flannel trousers and cardigan. The others stamped about and rubbed themselves to keep warm in their summer-holiday-on-the-equator clothes. The wise old Indians wrapped their capes closer about them and left the train at each little station, following the plumes of their white breath into the strange night with the glowing, moon-bright volcanoes still showing far, far away in the distance. It was quite dark now. The train was very late. Nine hours late. Not for Quito. Only for Riobamba, the big city, with a dandy nickname for itself. Riobamba is called the Sleeping Sultan of the Andes. I wondered how it got this name. Maybe it was because it had never fulfilled its potential, like they called Russia and China sleeping giants. Riobamba was perfectly placed to be a big, important city. The Incas, indeed, tried it out as the capital of their Northern Empire but that didn't work. The Spaniards did the same with the same results.

Its only claim now, I suppose, is as the headquarters of the railway line.

In a splendid turn-of-the-century building, a most elaborate and ornate building, they run the railway from Riobamba, trying to get very upset and excited about the train being late when, of course, the train is always late. The railway headquarters in Riobamba is a marvellous, working railway museum, or so, at least, Godfrey Pyecroft, the railway buff, kept telling us. The equipment they use is eighty-years old, the original gear, dating from the very time they opened the line, with the Presidente's beautiful young daughter, Señorita America Alfaro, daintily hammering in a golden spike, to show that the line was, in 1908, at long last done. Her father, the famous general, revolutionary, and man of progress, a few years later ran into trouble with the old guard, the Church and the grandees, who really ran things. One morning a mob turned up outside the beautiful Presidential Palace in Quito, dragged the Presidente out into the lovely square in the middle of town, hitched him up between two wild horses and unglamorously pulled him apart. Time vindicated the Presidente however. There is a statue to him now along the line. The Presidente looks like his old self again, all in one piece.

It's funny to think that on a journey of only 288 miles you have to stay overnight. But that's the way of steam. We got off in Riobamba. Old Godders knew, he said, of an absolutely wizard place not far away, much better than any local hotel, an old hacienda of one of the leading Conquistadors which was still the home of the old Spaniard's descendants but where you could stay the night. So we hired a car and drove off into scenery looking very much like Switzerland and at some dreadful hour drove down a long avenue between towering eucalyptus trees, moaning in the wind high above us, to this grand hacienda. Five hundred years ago the old Spaniards had brought Spain with them to the New World; and put a wall around it. And here it was, the home of the inheritors of the Conquistadors, the Lasso brothers, Don Patricio and Don Bolivar, direct descendants of Juan Sandoval, a Captain from Castile, who had married the beautiful sister of Atahualpa, the Inca Emperor. This hacienda was the prize they had spilled their own and so much Indian blood for, handed down through generations of Sandovals and Lassos, all carefully recorded the way the rich always are about their genealogy.

A beautiful place it was, full of playing fountains, sweet-smelling gardens, fine horses, dark-eyed, well-scrubbed Indian parlourmaids, and one of the most beautiful churches in Latin America: a family chapel, right out of *Brideshead Revisited* back home on the telly in England. They greeted us like proper Spaniards and laid on a big dinner in a great, long room and we, being all proper Anglo-Saxons of the very best sort, all got roaring drunk, acting like the appalling undergraduates that we spiritually were, with our chairs bent backwards and our feet up on the edge of the shiny, brown-as-highly-polished boots table.

'It's a great place, is Latin America,' said Witherspoon. 'They think all Englishmen are Eton an' Oxford an' bloody Brigade o' Guards. You can get away wi' murder if you're a proper Englishman in Latin America today.'

Pyecroft, who *was* Eton, Oxford and Brigade of Guards, looked immeasurably sad about this intelligence from Witherspoon. Pickerstaff laughed like a maniac about something he remembered somebody saying as he got on the train back in Guayaquil which he couldn't quite remember but, he assured us, it was ryahly scandalously funny.

We almost missed the train in Riobamba the morning after that night before. 'It really wasn't a bad night,' old Godders said. 'It reminded me of one of those really good nights at Oxford when you popped up to London and had such a good time that it took you two days to remember where you had parked the car.'

It might not have been such a bad idea to have missed the train in Riobamba for we left that marvellous old steam locomotive there. The steam train only takes you as far as Riobamba and then turns about and heads back down the coast. Looking at the hideous diesel that would take us on to Quito I had a great desire to turn back and ride the steam engine back down over those fantastic mountain peaks and chug down through the green-walled valleys of the Chan Chan to the seamy Joseph Conrad port city of *Nostromo*.

But Quito lay ahead and I wanted to see the journey to the end, follow in the steps of the Conquistadors, and see, too, the marvel of Quito, with its eighty-six gold-encrusted churches. But the contraption that was going to take us there didn't look up to much. Maybe it was fast and efficient but there was not an ounce of romance about it. This was something called the autoferro. It was merely a bus body, from Baltimore, Maryland, it turned out, which had been welded onto a diesel engine.

The marvellous Indians, who had filled our train coming up from the sea, did not, it seemed, travel any further than Riobamba. They were not going on to Quito. Instead we joined up with teenagers. They were well-off Ecuadorian children, loud and noisy as teenagers everywhere. They played their transistors loud, singing along to the dreadful din and even dancing, albeit in a timid, embarrassed manner, to the music in the aisle of the autoferro.

The other tourists were not taking the autoferro. The Ecuadorian auntie had a car waiting for her in Riobamba and was driving to Quito. What the

The autoferro about to pass the stationary Consolidation 44

Germans were doing I did not know. Probably they had rented a car to take them to Quito. Or they were going to return to Guayaquil by steam, in the hope of keeping awake this time round.

Old Godders was going back on the footplate. We tried to talk him into coming on to Quito with us, holding out the prospect of yet another undergraduate sort of night of beastly drunkenness, but he looked at the autoferro and smiled contemptuously at the twentieth century sitting there, all high gloss, shimmering silver, so unlike the grimy engines that he loved so dearly.

But we climbed high again on the autoferro and saw some beautiful sights, Alpine scenery, with the train speeding down long, trim avenues of fir-trees, and passed many sparkling, fast-flowing bits of water just made for great, thumping trout so large that you'd need a very heavy leader, a 2X or something like that. I wished I had taken along my rods, so I could ask the driver to stop and let me off. Maybe just one fish, having escaped the poaching Indians with their explosives, was waiting for me in there.

Now if you go to Guayaquil and suddenly find that you must go on to Quito you do not have to take a romantic and slow journey like I did. You can, indeed, do the whole trip on the autoferro and you will see the same sort of fine sights that I saw from the window of the old steam-hauled train. You might even meet some boon companions. But you cannot ride the footplate over the roof of the world on the autoferro. No, the driver sits inside, just like a proper, modern bus driver; he even collects the fares. And to share a bottle of wine and laugh out loud at the antics of a Pickerstaff or a Witherspoon on the autoferro would be very unseemly: conduct which might lead to a breach of the peace. There is absolutely nothing whatsoever Wild West or frontiersman about the autoferro. It is a clean, well-lighted, drip-dry, stay-pressed sort of a contraption: bullying, intrusive, a busy little engine, thoroughly, offensively modern, a right go-getter.

Out the window I saw the hacienda, looking rich and old time in the merry mountain sunlight. Some horsemen rode out, down that long avenue of tall trees. I saw a straggling line of them, with the man out front in the lead riding his horse like all the proper Spaniards do. He was trotting but he was not rising to the trot. In England you will only ever see the military men doing that. Behind him I could tell, even at this great distance, that the rest of them were not proper Spaniards, not the true descendants of the Conquistadors, just from the way they rode. They were not trotting even, but cantering along like riff-raff.

But the sight of that Spaniard on horseback not rising to the trot was a good old-fashioned sight. One fine day those old Spaniards rode out just like that, trotted up the hill, just to the spot where our bumptious little engine now was, and looked down and saw they were in sight of Quito, the Light of America, the city of Inca gold.

Sebastian de Benalcazar, as tough a looking old fellow as you are ever likely to meet, has a statue of himself standing in Riobamba, gazing out in the direction of Quito. Inside the railway station is a photograph on the wall of the main entrance of old Archer Harman, the hard-nosed old Yankee devil who brought the railway to Ecuador. They could have been brothers, those bearded two, Sebastian and Archer. Both of them were out for money. Greed drove them on but, in the way of these things, it did not work out the way they thought it would. No riches were made out of the railways in Ecuador. Today it is easier to fly between Guayaquil and Quito. That's how the rich Ecuadorians do it, and the snappy international businessmen for whom time is money. Archer Harman's railway is for the poor. It links the country for them. It is cheap enough for them to ride down on it to see the sea or go up on it to see the mountains; and cheap enough, too, to carry the sort of things from the sea and the jungles – fruit, fish, sugar-cane, newspapers – that they would not have in the high mountains without the train. Archer Harman, however, I am sure, never had this sort of charity in mind.

The Conquistadors brought Europe with them. Like the Aztecs in Mexico, the Incas in Peru and Ecuador were a race of conquerors themselves. The Spaniards were simply a superior master race. There is no truth in the myth that the Indians of Ecuador were a happy people before the Spaniards came. They had been conquered by the Incas only a relatively short time before.

When Benalcazar, with his 200 horsemen, marched on Quito, along the Royal Road which the autoferro runs alongside, they cut their way through 50,000 Indians. At one battle they faced 15,000 Incas. The Virgin appeared in the sky, for the first time in Ecuador but definitely not the last time, and directed the Spaniards' field of action. It was a splendid victory. A curious people these old Spaniards. They did not, as any modern general would, press home this victory and ride on Quito. Instead they stopped and built a church. That was in 1534. It is the oldest church in Ecuador. It still stands. Indeed, it is the same church my Indian travelling companion spoke to me of, the one which commemorates that fire on the train in 1957 when the Virgin appeared in the sky in answer to the prayers of the pious brakeman.

Greedy for gold, pious for their religion, these old Spaniards had ridden down on Quito, the Inca summer capital. Once there they found a ghost town. The Inca army had fled, taking all the population and all the gold with them. We saw Quito laid out before us now, from the same hills as the Spaniards had looked down on it. The teenagers in the autoferro were singing some ghastly pop song, it was in Spanish but it was American, they were happy and right at home in their homogenised culture and they were, you knew in your bones, the future of Ecuador. The journey from Riobamba on the autoferro had taken six hours and the evening light was just fading over the roof tops of Quito as we came down on it in the hoof prints of the Conquistadors. Suddenly the whole city was laid out before us, bathed in two lights, one golden and one blue, with all the fountains of the city's squares looking magical in the curious evening light, and the golden domes and roofs of Quito's eighty-six churches as beautiful as Florence or Venice or any of those fabled Italian cities.

I was glad I had started this journey at mass because I saw it had been a sort of pilgrimage to a holy place, a city that was a shrine to those greedy old Spaniards. They hadn't really come here to spread their religion. They had come for gold. But somehow it hadn't worked out that way and by some trick of fate their base instinct had been transformed. Finding no city of gold, the Spaniards had to build one of their own.

'Ah know a place in Quito,' said Witherspoon, 'where you can get steak 'n' chips.'

'Ha!' said Pickerstaff, '— zzz – Is zas so?'

And then we proceeded out on the most riotous night and then, in the morning, decided to do it all again – three men on a footplate – riding down to see old Godders in Guayaquil.

NOTES ON THE CONTRIBUTORS

RUSSELL CHAMBERLIN is a professional writer, the author of more than twenty books on different forms of social history. Although he knows Europe well (six of his books are directly concerned with the Italian Renaissance) the journey described here was his first visit to Portugal. A non-driver and a dedicated hater of cars, he believes firmly that public transport is the only solution to the monster that is throttling our cities, and that the railway is the ideal form of such transport. He is currently working on a book tracing the history of travel in England from Chaucer to George Orwell.

COLIN GARRATT is probably the only photographer and writer in the world professionally engaged in documenting the end of the steam age. In 1969, he abandoned a marketing career to begin his self-imposed task and now, fifteen years later, at the age of forty-four, has covered some fifty countries.

Colin's work – which is largely self-funded – is a desperate race against time as the great age of steam slowly fades into oblivion. Although he has written and illustrated sixteen books, and is a frequent contributor to national magazines, Colin is equally well known for his personal lectures and Audio Visual Roadshows which tour the country each year. 'The Dragons of Sugar Island' was Colin's second TV film, the first being a BBC1 *Omnibus* documentary about his work.

As and when his inevitable 120-hour working week relents a little, Colin dreams of spearheading a national campaign to restore Britain's railways to their former glory and importance. Colin Garratt

also has a passionate concern for the conservation of wildlife and harbours a deep anger over the creeping destruction of the English countryside.

Colin lives in the tiny Leicestershire village of Newton Harcourt and his study overlooks the bridge from which he watched his first train in 1949.

PETER HILLMORE is Pendennis of *The Observer*. After reading English at Oxford, he joined the staff of the *Guardian*. During his meteoric rise sideways he wrote variously about industry, the Far East and general features before finally editing *The Guardian* Diary column for two years. He then joined London Weekend Television to produce a late-night current affairs programme full of a skilful combination of meaningful trivia. He joined the staff of *The Observer* in 1982. He divides his time between Gloucestershire and London.

SIMON HOGGART had no particular interest in trains, but a great interest in exploring northern Canada, which is why he enthusiastically agreed to write the commentary for the *Great Little Railways* programme on the White Pass and Yukon Route. He came away loving the area, the railway itself and the infectious delight of many of the people who work for it. He was raised in north and east Yorkshire, moved to the Midlands with his family and went to King's College, Cambridge. He joined *The Guardian* as a graduate trainee and later went to Belfast as Northern Ireland correspondent. In 1973 he moved to London as a political writer and in 1981 joined the staff of *The Observer*. He also has a weekly column in *Punch* and has taken part in a number of TV and radio programmes, most of which seem doomed to disappear from the screens, possibly as a result of his involvement. He is married and lives in Notting Hill, London.

STANLEY REYNOLDS, the Literary Editor of *Punch*, is a confirmed train traveller. Before he joined *Punch* he wrote a humorous column for *The Guardian*, whose staff he joined in 1963, and delighted readers with his articles on train travel, particularly long, summer jaunts to cricket matches with Cedric, the old Yorkshire groundsman, and Binky Ainsworth, the Oxford blue. His love of the little electric lines of suburbia is as passionate as Sir John Betjeman's although, like all romantics, steam is his first love. Born in New England in 1934 he has lived most of his life in England and now spends his time on a train between a flat in the City and a cottage in Oxfordshire where he messes about with a rowing boat stroking from pub to pub. Due to the excessive foolishness of publishers his brilliant satirical novels of the 1960s are out of print, but they contained nothing about trains although there is a dandy little Mogul 2–6–0 in the novel he is now writing after more than a decade of disgusting sloth.

LYN WEBSTER's great-grandfather drove the train which took Queen Victoria on her holidays in the highlands, and her grandfather drove a little engine underground in the pits. Her earliest memories are of travelling up to Scotland on the *Flying Scotsman* when it was a steam engine.

She left Newnham College, Cambridge, in 1971 with a first in English, and since then has worked in radio and television, doing every sort of job and ending up as a producer/director. She produced the comedy series *Revolting Women*, which became a cult amongst the under-eighteens but seems to have baffled everyone else, and she has made many films for BBC2's *Brass Tacks* on social issues such as abortion and solitary confinement in prisons. She has just left the BBC to work as a freelance producer/writer and is at the moment completing a metaphysical adventure story which may end up as a novel or a film, or both.

MICHAEL WOOD was born in Manchester and educated at Manchester Grammar School and at Oriel College, Oxford, where he read Modern History. He held undergraduate and postgraduate scholarships and in 1972 won the University's English Essay prize. His research work was in tenth-century history. Since 1976 he has worked for the BBC. He wrote and presented the *In Search of . . .* series and has written a book based on the programmes called *In Search of the Dark Ages*. He also wrote and presented one of the programmes in the series *Great Railway Journeys of the World* and contributed to a book which accompanied the series, and has contributed to the BBC series, *River Journeys*, and the accompanying book. Among his forthcoming publications is a full-length study of King Athelstan and his age, and a book which traces the development of Aegean archaeology, *In Search of the Trojan War*.

PICTURE CREDITS

INDEX